The Complete
Q&A Job
Interview Book
Third Edition

Other books by Jeffrey G. Allen, J.D., C.P.C.

HOW TO TURN AN INTERVIEW INTO A JOB
(also available on audiocassette)

FINDING THE RIGHT JOB AT MIDLIFE

THE PLACEMENT STRATEGY HANDBOOK

THE EMPLOYEE TERMINATION HANDBOOK

PLACEMENT MANAGEMENT

SURVIVING CORPORATE DOWNSIZING

THE PERFECT JOB REFERENCE

THE NATIONAL PLACEMENT LAW CENTER
   FEE COLLECTION GUIDE

THE PERFECT FOLLOW-UP METHOD TO GET THE JOB

JEFF ALLEN'S BEST: THE RESUME

JEFF ALLEN'S BEST: GET THE INTERVIEW

JEFF ALLEN'S BEST: WIN THE JOB

COMPLYING WITH THE ADA: HIRING AND
   EMPLOYING THE DISABLED

SUCCESSFUL JOB SEARCH STRATEGIES FOR THE DISABLED

THE CAREER TRAP

THE RESUME MAKEOVER

EXECUTIVE TEMPORARIES

The Complete Q&A Job Interview Book
Third Edition

Jeffrey G. Allen

John Wiley & Sons

New York • Chichester • Weinheim • Brisbane • Singapore • Toronto

Copyright © 2000 by Jeffrey G. Allen. All rights reserved.

Published by John Wiley & Sons, Inc.

Published simultaneously in Canada.

This publication is designed to provide accurate and authoritative information in regard to the subject matter covered. It is sold with the understanding that the publisher is not engaged in rendering professional services. If professional advice or other expert assistance is required, the services of a competent professional person should be sought.

Library of Congress Cataloging-in-Publication Data:
Allen, Jeffrey G., 1943–
    The complete Q & A job interview book / Jeffrey G. Allen.—3rd ed.
      p. cm.
    Includes bibliographical references and index.
    ISBN 0-471-39145-X (pbk. : alk. paper)
    1. Employment interviewing.   I. Title: Complete Q and A job interview book.   II. Title: Complete question and answer job interview book.   III. Title.
HF5549.5.I6 A43   2000
650.14—dc21   00-033006

Printed in the United States of America

10 9 8 7 6 5 4 3 2 1

With appreciation . . .

To my wife, Bev;
to our daughter, Angela;
and to Louann Werksma;
for their capable assistance in the research
and preparation of the script manuscript.

Contents

Introduction

A job interview is a screen test, an act. Getting hired depends almost completely on the actor factor. If you know your lines, perfect your delivery, and dress for the part, you'll get hired. If you don't, you won't. No retakes. No bit parts.

For almost a decade, I was behind a personnel director's desk, interviewing applicants of every age, stage, and wage, every day (and night—in my sleep). I've probably read every book on how to interview. I've taken courses on it. I've even trained supervisors on how to do it.

I rapped nonstop about interviewing techniques: directive or nondirective, specific or general, closed-ended or open-ended, structured or unstructured, restricted or unrestricted, window, choice, hypothetical, theoretical, interpretive, leading, loaded, stress, interrogation, machine-gun, multiple, double, curiosity, and so on.

Interviewing is a welcome break for supervisors and keeps a lot of personnellers off the unemployment line. But studying interviewing techniques is a total waste of time for a serious job seeker. At best, studying them will get you tired long before you're hired. At worst, it will intimidate you. Interviewing hasn't changed since Laurel hired Hardy. It's just as comical as it has always been.

Now you can memorize the script in advance. There are only so many questions that can be asked and only so many ways to ask them. Oh, there might be minor variations—like the accent of the interviewer, his or her tone of voice, or a pause here and there. Experienced jobgetters appreciate them. Otherwise, they'd undoubtedly start snoring before the offers were extended.

Because interviews are so predictable, they're *controllable*. Only the places and faces change—not the words. And you can have them all embedded in your subconscious, ready for instant replay at the drop of an interesting job lead.

I know—you think background, qualifications, or experience have something to do with getting hired. You're right—not about the *job*, though. About *interviewing*! The director only knows what you show. That's why the actor factor is so critical.

Twenty-five years ago, I developed the only measure that counts: the interview-to-offer ratio. If you ask enough people, you'll find the ratio averages twelve to one: It takes *twelve* interviews for the average person to get *one* job offer. That means for every person who intuitively knows how to get hired every time (or uses our techniques), some walking wounded is limping into his or her *twenty-fourth* interview. For every two people who know, there's someone being carried into his or her *forty-eighth*, showing battle scars and telling war stories. Destroyed, not employed.

After a while, these folks live with a self-fulfilling prophecy: rejection. They might as well just call the interviewer and say, "I'm canceling the interview. Your time is too valuable to waste with me." They're destined to flub their lines from the time the first board claps.

Tragic. Even more tragic when that interview-to-offer ratio will tumble down for *anyone* who'll just follow the programmed interview system automatically. It's nothing more than preparing that amazing computer between your ears to signal your mouth and limbs to move in the right way at the right time.

Unlike your conscious mind, which understands, judges, and controls (thinks), your subconscious mind stores information. If you give it the right input (images and cues), the output (words and actions) will be right, too.

The input about interviewing that is now stored back there in your subconscious is probably based on a few random encounters when you were looking for a job. You were nervous, unprepared, and probably don't even consciously remember how you reflexively responded. In fact, applicants forget *90 percent* of the dialogue within hours after leaving an interviewer's office! Some are lucky if they even remember their own names when they leave.

This is no way to learn how to respond to something so predictable as an interview. There's no positive reinforcement—no disciplined practice, either. How unfortunate when your livelihood and personhood are on the line.

At first most people are afraid they'll be like a bionic with a broken brain and will just talk or move out of context. Not a chance. The subconscious just stores. Words and actions will happen naturally when the time is right. You'll adapt the delivery to your own vocabulary and mannerisms like any accomplished actor. That's why interviewers will never know you're using the system. They won't care, either. They want that job requisition off their desks and out of their lives for as long as possible. They'll even coach you if you know your lines.

Oh, maybe you have some moral problems with using the actor factor to your advantage and not being yourself. If so, I suggest you ask a past interviewer for the rating forms he or she used on you. It won't get you hired, but it will open your eyes wide to the games interviewers play and to how biased, unfair, and incorrect their snap judgments really are. Now you can work this to your advantage.

People who interview well are better employees, too. That's because they've learned how to *interact* on the job—to sell themselves and their ideas to others. They aren't en-slaved because they know they can always find another job. They're working because they *want* to. They're the ones who succeed in their careers: Positive interaction gets people hired, promoted, and recruited for better opportunities. They develop a loyal fan club, which follows them to the top.

All you're doing is taking the most random selection process imaginable and controlling it. That's right, *you're* in control! No, I don't recommend that you try to switch seats with the interviewer. You'll never have that much control. It's his or her office and decision (almost). After all, he or she can always yell, "Cut!"

So don't fight it. Just *do* it. Let it work for you. Then you won't want to fight it anyway. You'll feel great about yourself when you know you can knock any interview cold. You should. You have lifetime unemployment insurance and a su-percharged career.

Here's how to use the programmed interview technique to fast-forward your future:

1. Read the questions and answers to yourself once.

2. Customize the questions where necessary to apply to your background and target job.

3. Customize the answers where necessary to your vocabu-lary, background, and target job. (Just don't change them radically; each answer is carefully designed and tested to score the most points. The further you deviate from it, the more you risk.)

4. Prepare a cassette for yourself containing the most difficult questions for you to answer, leaving spaces on the tape to

read your answers aloud. (You can stop the tape occasionally to rehearse a particular response, but it is important to simulate an interview where the dialogue continues.)

5. Then, play the cassette at least three times a week for the next two weeks, sitting in front of a full-length mirror. Try to simulate an interview as closely as possible by using a table for a desk and adding other props. Don't stop the tape. Pay attention to your facial expressions, hand movements, and body language. Smile. Look the interviewer (you) in the eye. Try not to speak with your hands. Lean forward to make a point.

6. Use your driving, riding, or walking time to listen to the cassette and answer the questions. (You can just *think* the answers, but talking aloud to your imaginary friend will rivet your attention. Engaging your mouth when your brain is in gear is good practice.)

PREPARATION

If you want to come out of a job interview with an offer on the table, then for you the interview should begin as far in advance of the date and time of your appointment as possible. For starters you'll want to find out as much as you can prior to the big day about the company and the position you're applying for. And you'll need to find out what's considered appropriate dress and deportment at the company. These issues are not as clear-cut as they once were. Traditionally, standards had been set, which no one questioned. Both men and women were expected to dress conservatively (suits and ties for men and business suits or dresses for women). As to personal conduct, the standard advice was to be reserved and respectful and let the interviewer control the interview.

Today abiding by these standards certainly will stand you in good stead in many situations and professions; when you're in doubt, they can and should be considered your fallback position. But since the early 1980s, there is no single response to how to dress and behave in a job interview. In particular since the Internet has come into widespread use, with the concomitant explosion of e-commerce, job applicants may find themselves face to face with break-all-the-rules entrepreneurs as well as traditional business people—sometimes in the same day—who want and expect different things from job candidates. More than ever applicants must prepare themselves by researching the firms and people with positions to fill. Let's begin by discussing the importance of learning all you can about the company you'll be interviewing with.

It's What You Know

Unless you know someone at the company where you'll be interviewing, someone who can and is willing to share with you insider information, you have to reverse the adage "It's not what you know, it's who you know." To be confident going into an interview (which is a primary ingredient in making a good impression), you need to find out as much as you can about the company—and ideally the person or people—you'll be interviewing with. Fortunately, this has never been easier. Thanks to the Internet, and more specifically the World Wide Web, you can find out valuable information about most companies worldwide. No longer do you have to make difficult, sometimes embarrassing phone calls to receptionists or assistants and try to eke out any piece of information that might give you a leg up on the interview. No longer do you have to go to the library and track down articles in periodicals or newspapers in search of recent news on a company or person. Just log on to the Internet and the business world is at your fingertips—literally.

> **Note** If you don't have Internet access from your home, most libraries and schools now provide free service to the public.

It's How You Look

Since the 1980s, dress in the workplace has become almost universally more casual (with a few exceptions, such as the legal and investment brokerage professions); even doctors wear jeans or chinos under their lab coats (which aren't even always white anymore). What started as casual Fridays have become casual all days in many organizations. Perhaps prompted by the rapid and widespread emergence of high-tech companies, many of whose founding entrepreneurs considered themselves to be rebels against the tight-laced, suit-and-tie corporate world, the old rules of suits for men and dresses for women have, by and large, fallen by the wayside. Today most companies, large and small, have loosened their dress codes. To the job candidate, this raises difficult questions about how to dress for an interview. Do you dress the old-fashioned way, meant to show respect and to impress, or do you show your willingness to fit in by dressing as others in the company do? The answer is: It depends.

The following are some guideline questions to ask—and get answered—in advance of your scheduled interview.

How do the employees in your target company dress? Does there seem to be a standard, a dress code?

If you don't know the answer to this, you might just want to conduct some on-site casual research (assuming you are not traveling out of town to the interview). Hang out during rush hour or lunch hour at the company headquarters, for example, to see how people are dressed. A more direct and surefire approach is to call the human resources department at the company and ask someone there what the dress code is. Do not be embarrassed to ask this question. It is the job of human resources personnel to act as the go-betweens for the employer and employee candidates. They want to ensure they're not wasting the time of the interviewers by setting them up with inappropriate candidates, and they'll respect your desire to dress correctly.

And don't forget the Web; most companies how have web sites, and a good number of those sites include job opportunities sections or pages, where you might be able to get the information you need. In particular, if you're interviewing with a large corporation, you'll probably discover its web site goes into some detail about its recruitment procedures. Companies don't want to waste their time or yours, so they make this information readily available. Take advantage of all the sources available to you.

What if the company is so small it has no human resources department or no web site?

Today, it's highly unlikely that a company won't have one of these sources of information available, but if this is the case, chances are you'll have a preliminary screening interview, often by phone, either with the person you'll be meeting with at a later date or with his or her assistant. During that conversation, you may be able to ask about the company's dress code. If you feel it's inappropriate or uncomfortable to do so, err on the side of caution: Dress conservatively, in traditional business attire—suits for men and business suits or dresses for women.

What if I'm told it's okay to wear jeans?

Unless you're *absolutely sure* this is acceptable, don't do it. It's still safer to dress "up"; in general no interviewer is going to penalize you for being too neatly or conservatively dressed. I say "in general" because today this, too, can be tricky. Some companies today, in particular the innovative dot-coms, whose owners and executives prize creativeness and the entrepreneurial spirit, may be put off by someone who appears too traditional. Again, preparedness is key: Know the industry, know the company. Probably a safe level of dress for this type of company is somewhere between traditional and casual: for men, chinos, a shirt, tie, and sport coat; for women, slacks, shirt, and blazer.

It's How You Act

As important (perhaps even more so) as the clothes you wear is how you carry yourself and behave—your deportment. Probably the best way to tell you what to do is by telling you what not to do:

- Don't chew gum or smoke; don't bring food or a beverage (even water). If you're asked if you'd like something to drink, accept if you want, but don't presume it's all right to bring refreshments with you.

- When your interviewer extends his or her hand to shake in greeting, don't limp-fish your grip; make it firm, full of self-confidence. Make solid eye contact with each person you meet.

- Don't sit down until invited to do so. Then, sit upright; don't slouch or sprawl.

- Don't give in to the tendency to talk with your hands if you, like many other people, do this when you're nervous. Hold your hands in your lap if you have to, but don't wave them around as punctuation to your remarks. Your interviewer will focus on your hands, not on what you're saying.

- As much as possible, refrain from interjecting your comments with uhs, you knows, um, and the like. It's no sin to pause and say nothing while gathering your thoughts.

- Don't take the ball and run with it, which means don't talk so much that you dominate the interview. Don't anticipate what the interviewer is going to say or ask, and most important, don't interrupt. Likewise, don't try to demonstrate you know more than the person interviewing you! Remember this is a conversation between people, not a soapbox from which you are expected to recite your knowledge and capabilities.

- If you're being interviewed by more than one person, focus on whoever is speaking or directing a question. Do not look only at the person you know to be in charge. Employers want to be assured that you are comfortable dealing with employees at all levels of the company. Treat everyone as your client or customer.

Theoretically, the number of questions you can be asked in an interview is unlimited. This is because there are unlimited word combinations in the English language. However, our inventory of thousands of questions was consolidated and organized into the chapters that follow. We carefully chose questions that are generic enough to cover the entire range of interview subjects and then selected those designed to elicit "KO (knockout) factors"—the ones that have you down for the count on the interviewer's carpet. Knowing how to respond to the questions we chose—programming your mind with effective answers—will enable you to naturally respond to any variations that arise. Unconsciously, your brain will scan your database for your input and instantly signal your mouth, eyes, limbs, and torso to respond in unison with maximum impact. Don't worry about overrehearsing. You can't. You either know your lines or you don't. Once you do, you'll never forget them when you hear the cue.

Once you start auditioning, you'll feel more confident. You *should*. You know the script. You're computer literate, too. In the actual interviews, you'll be a superstar, receiving Oscar offers time after time. Talent scouts (recruiters) will call you an MPC (most placeable candidate). Your biggest worries will be taking the time for interviews and deciding which offers deserve Academy-Award-winning acceptances. All superstars must face these decisions. Ah, the price you pay.

Practice your lines, go through your dress rehearsals, and watch your self-esteem increase as you shine above the cast of thousands. From script to screen test, you'll be headed straight for that office with the star on the door.

No more understudy roles. Straight up. An anxious public awaits. Roll 'em—and—*knock 'em dead!*

Chapter

1

Personal and Family Data

DELIVERY

Of all the questions you'll be asked, personal and family ones appear to be the most statistical. For this reason, most job-seekers answer them in a static way, with name, rank, and serial number.

They're also often emotionally charged because interviewers ask about personal perils, family feuds, and status symbols. Therefore, rehearsing your lines is particularly important because what you *say* is as important as what you *convey*.

While most of the questions in this area have only marginal value in determining your qualifications to perform a specific job, you must get *past* them so you can get down to business with the interviewer. That's why they're called "KO" factors. Wrong answers mean *knock out* in Round 1; right answers will keep you in the ring for a while.

Personal and family items are invariably at the top of resumes, on the front of application forms, and at the beginning of interview checklists. Because these documents are the cue cards used in the actual interview, expect the questions in Act 1, Round 1.

If first impressions really count (and they *really* do to overworked people who are interviewing), then now is your chance to shine. Most film critics will tell you they lock into a review within five minutes. If they watch longer, it's either to enjoy the show or to justify their negative rating. That's why lawyers often see judges writing their decisions from the bench soon after the opening statements. Yours will, too. Your judge is overworked.

Greet the interviewer with the Magic Four Hello:

1. *A smile.* If you can't fake it, just think about how lucky the interviewer is to be meeting you.

2. *Direct eye contact.* If it's too much for you, look at the bridge of the interviewer's nose.

3. *Introduce yourself.* Say, "Hi, I'm (first name) (last name). It's a pleasure meeting you."

4. *A firm but gentle handshake.* Rehearse. No live shark; no dead flounder.

Then, once you're on the set (the interviewer's office):

1. Head for the chair on your favored side (right if you are right-handed, left if you are left-handed). If you're ambidextrous, you can take center stage. Just be sure there's a chair behind you.

2. Stand there until you're asked to be seated. (If you're not asked, it's probably because you've *already* drawn an SRO audience!)

Now, sit up straight, feet on the floor (women may cross their legs), and look the interviewer in the eye.

Lights . . . Camera . . .

SCRIPT

Just the Facts

The first seven questions that follow might have appeared on the employment application you completed prior to the interview. Even if you answered them already, be prepared again with short, direct, upbeat answers. Most applicants answer either with statistics (bad) or excuses (worse). With a little practice, you'll really shine when it counts most—at the beginning.

1. What are your parents' occupations?

(Think your answer through. Avoid saying anything negative, like "My father was just a janitor" or "My mother didn't work." Show pride in your background and heritage, even if you have come to regard it as very humble: "My father was a custodial supervisor, and my mother ran a busy home."

Be careful about overstating, too. Avoid an answer like "My father is the leading brain surgeon in the state and my mother is a retired Superior Court judge." In such cases, "My father is a surgeon and my mother is an attorney and former judge" positions you properly.)

My father is a _____, and my mother is a _____.

2. Do you live with your parents?

(It's okay if you do. Even mature adults are finding it financially beneficial to share expenses with their parents. Give the impression that you made a responsible financial decision.)

Yes, I moved back in with my parents after I discovered that over half my net income was being used to pay for rent and utilities. We have an economic arrangement that allows me to save for my future, while I'm around to help them maintain our home. We all benefit, and we have been able to develop a strong friendship as three adults.

3. **Were you in the military service? Where and when?**

   (If yes, give dates and where stationed. Mention briefly any training or experience that relates directly to your target job.)

   I served as a _____ in the _____ from _____ to_____.

   OR (if no)

   I was never in the military.

4. **What is the year and model of your car?**

   (If the job for which you are applying requires you to use your own car for company business and if you really are riding a set of wheels, mention the make and model of the reliable car you intend to buy soon. After all, you *do, don't* you?)

   I own a _____.

   OR

   I will be buying a _____.

5. Do you own or rent your home?

(This is one of those questions that attempts to establish your stability. The translation is "Are you a responsible member of the community?" Answer briefly and honestly. If you are renting while you save to buy your own home, mention where you've been looking. If you haven't, start now with a call to a local real estate agent.)

(I/We) purchased our home in _____(name of town) in _____(year).

OR

(I am/We are) currently renting a (House/unit) in _____(name of town), but (I'm/we're) looking for (my/our) own home in the area.

6. How far do you live from this company?

(If you currently live farther away than what would be considered a reasonable commuting distance, you might mention that you would be willing to locate nearer the company's offices if hired.)

I clocked it on my way here today. I'm exactly 10 miles door to door, and it took me 17 minutes to get here. A breeze.

OR

The ride here today was 40 miles. With moderate traffic, it took almost an hour. I don't mind commuting that far twice a day—I like to get an early start on my day anyway. If I were hired, however, I would probably investigate the real estate market in the immediate area.

7. Do you speak a foreign language?

(If you speak another language fluently, by all means say so. This is an asset. However, if you took Spanish or French in school but cannot remember more than two or three phrases, simply mention that you understand the language better than you speak it. Try this answer:)

I studied _____ (Spanish/French/German) in _____ (high school/college) and enjoyed it. I'd like to get some language tapes and increase my fluency.

RELATIONSHIPS AND HOME LIFE

You're probably aware that certain questions cannot be asked by an employer prior to hiring an applicant. These include questions that directly or indirectly probe race, color, religion, national origin, age, gender, marital status, physical handicap, medical condition, arrest information or other unlawful criteria.

In spite of the law, illegal questions get asked every day, and company attitudes and interviewer prejudices creep into every personnel situation. You can choose not to respond, you can tell the interviewer you intend to file a charge of discrimination, or you can lecture to the interviewer about civil rights. These things might make you feel better momentarily, but they will likely result in an *apology*, not an *offer*. Wouldn't you rather answer the question, get the job, and change the employer's attitude? Everybody will win if you get hired.

8. How much time do you spend with your family?

(Be careful to project a balanced attitude here. This can be a touchy subject. You might be dealing with an interviewer who is work oriented and lives by the credo: Work is not only the way to make a living; it's the way to make a life. Or you might be talking to one who recognizes the importance of family. Before you answer, scope out the situation: Look around the office for family photos, desk accessories made by children, and the like. The following is your basic generic answer. Customize it as necessary.)

I suppose I spend an average amount. My family is important to me. My great relationship with them gives me the best reason in the world to succeed in my career. In that way, they are an inspiration.

I have a responsibility to my job as well as to my family, since I've made a strong commitment to both. I like to be there for them when they need me, but they also understand and accept the commitment I have made to my work. So I spend my time accordingly.

9. In your opinion, what makes a happy marriage?

(Another loaded question. Even if unmarried, you have probably developed some ideas on this subject. Again, keep it balanced.)

I think a good marriage is based on mutual respect and trust, with a lot of sharing, communicating, and giving. If you can't express your feelings in a sensitive but candid way, your marriage will undoubtedly suffer.

Learning to communicate effectively with and to understand the needs of another in your personal relationships teaches you how to get along better on the job. And a good marriage frees you to be more successful in your work. All the successful people I've known have had their personal lives in order. So a happy marriage is worth the effort.

10. Who is the boss in your family?

(Unfortunately, there are still interviewers out there asking this type of question. Remember, avoid an angry reaction. Allow for the possibility that the interviewer is just trying to lure you into saying something without thinking. Just smile confidently, and say:)

We operate our family on democratic principles, with the adults making ultimate decisions on what is best for the children. My (husband/wife) and I are equal partners.

11. **Is your spouse employed? Will there be a conflict?**

(This is one of those logical but unnecessary questions that is often asked. If you answer it in a neutral way, the interviewer will go on to something else. Yet, if you indicate there is a conflict, it could reduce your chances of being hired. The following answer usually works well:)

Yes, my _____ (husband/wife) is a _____ (computer programmer/astronaut) for _____. We have always been a two-career couple, and we have made the arrangements necessary to accommodate our careers.

12. **What contributed to your divorce? What have you learned from this experience?**

(This *is* getting personal. It might not be within the bounds of good taste; but worded this way, the question is probably legal.)

We married very young and made some mistakes we didn't know how to correct. We lost touch with each other, and eventually it was too late to salvage anything. I've learned that, to earn respect and honesty, you have to communicate openly and be prepared to *give* honesty and respect. It was a painful lesson, and I have no intention of repeating it.

13. Describe your relationship with your children.

I was surprised by my reaction to _____ (motherhood/fatherhood). My _____ (husband/wife) and I waited a long time to have kids and weren't sure what kind of parents we would be. We have come to appreciate our children's day-to-day activities, and sometimes we wonder what we ever did for fun before they were born.

14. What child care arrangements have been made for your children?

(While this question was rarely, if ever, asked of a male applicant in the past, it is and should be an employer's concern no matter who is applying for the job. Today, more than half the children in the United States are being raised by single heads of household or have two working parents, and the lack of quality child care is a problem that can intrude on any parent's work life. Letting the interviewer know you have worked out a solid solution will show your sense of responsibility to those important people in your life, as well as to your work.)

Our children attend an excellent nursery school and day care center near our home. The youngest is there all day, and the oldest is dropped off after school. Usually, my _____ (husband/wife) picks them up at night, while I have responsibility for morning drop-off. If work commitments prevent both of us from getting there by 6 o'clock, when they close, there is a responsible neighbor who picks them up, brings them home, and prepares dinner for them.

Personal Management

These questions relate to the ways in which you arrange your personal life. The philosophy behind them is that personal decisions provide clues to your attitude and behavior on the job. Be prepared with answers that will show responsible, mature attitudes and actions now, even if there are some hazy spots in your past.

15. Do you keep and follow a personal budget?

(Any of the three alternatives given, all of which reflect responsibility and good judgment, are acceptable.)

Yes.

OR

Not item by item, but I don't live beyond my means.

OR

Generally, yes. I've intentionally allowed for flexibility to take advantage of good investment opportunities or exceptional savings on household purchases.

16. Do you own a life insurance policy?

Yes.

OR

No, I don't believe life insurance would be an efficient use of my money now. When I have dependents for whom I am responsible, I will buy life insurance. Right now, I prefer to invest my money.

17. Do you have a savings plan?

(Almost everyone has a savings *plan*, even if they have only one account with a minimum balance. He or she didn't ask you if you *followed* your plan. So the answer will invariably be "Yes." If applicable, you can add the following:)

Yes, I contribute _____ (5 percent/10 percent) of my net pay to a regular savings account.

18. Are you in debt?

(Ouch! This is another one of those I wish I didn't have to prepare you to answer.)

Well, I have a _____ (mortgage/ auto loan/charge card balance), but my personal balance sheet is definitely in the black. I don't extend my credit beyond what I can afford to pay.

19. Have you ever been refused a bond?

(If not, then "No." Period. If yes, consider carefully the reason, and what has changed in your personal life since that time. Explain the situation briefly and sincerely.)

Yes, that happened in _____ (year) due to _____
_____.

However, I _____.

20. Do you have a valid driver's license?

Yes.

OR

No, but if this job requires someone who drives, I would apply for a license as soon as possible.

21. Have you ever had a driver's license revoked? Why?

(If no, then the answer is simple. If yes, hopefully the circumstances that led to such an occurrence are long in your past. Your best bet is to think carefully about your own personal situation, and find a way of presenting it in the most positive light. For example:)

When I was a teenager, I ran up some points, and my license was suspended briefly. I have held my driver's license now for _____ years without a single moving violation in that time.

22. When was your last physical examination?

It was _____ (date), and my health is excellent.

23. Do you have any chronic health conditions we should consider?

(If not, then simply answer "No." The question is illegal, and the interviewer is asking for your opinion. The only time you should answer this question positively is if you do have a condition that will become evident in a preemployment physical, like diabetes. In that case, you might answer:)

Nothing that would interfere with my work performance. I have had diabetes for ____ years, but I control it very successfully and unobtrusively. It has never become an issue in my work; and, aside from my family, only my doctor knows. It isn't a secret—it just has nothing to do with performing on the job.

Chapter

2

Educational Background

DELIVERY

Although not as sensitive an area as personal and family questions, educational questions also cause applicants to trip when they make their grand entrances.

Degree delirium reached epidemic proportions in the United States during the 1960s and 1970s. After many casualties (and fatalities), industry has finally realized that *experience in thinking* doesn't necessarily correlate to *ability at doing*. Experience at *doing* is a much more accurate measure. If you doubt this, just look at the early films of most veteran actors.

I discussed the value of initials after your name in *Finding the Right Job at Midlife.*

> During a recent tour, I found myself in front of a microphone on an all-night radio talk show somewhere west of New York. I ran out of fingers counting the number of interviews that day and was due to catch a plane to the next city. Since they're so much easier to catch when they're on the ground, the host announced that the next call would be the last. The called asked, "What does the 'J.D., C.P.C.' after your name mean?" Of course, the straight answer would have been, "Juris Doctor and Certified Placement Counselor." But I just couldn't be straight under the circumstances. As I removed the headset and stood up to leave, my candid reply said it all: "The 'J.D.' stands for 'Just Do It!', and the 'C.P.C.' stands for 'Courage, Persistence, and Confidence!'"

So unless you're applying for a job that *requires* a specialized course of study for *entry* (lawyer, doctor, *certified* public accountant, etc.), don't waste a good worry about that piece of paper. In fact, be careful about accentuating unrelated education—it can pull you off the stage like a hook from the wings.

Don't falsify anything, and be sure to indicate any other names you used in school. (Sorry, Farrah Rambo Einstein is already taken.) These can be checked easily and usually are.

Instead, tell how your education ties in with:

1. A *business* approach.

2. *Self-discipline.*

3. The *target job* you're after.

SCRIPT

1. What college did you attend?

I went to _____ in _____.

2. Why did you attend that particular college?

I chose _____ because of its competitive atmosphere and the good reputation of the _____ School. Although I could have attended other colleges, this one emphasized practical, job-related courses and student participation in activities related to their specific career plans.

Many of my friends found themselves going to colleges their parents had chosen, but I set my own educational and career goals. _____ might have been a little more expensive than some of the other colleges, but this forced me to work harder because I helped pay my own way.

I'm pleased with my decision. I relied on my instincts, and they paid off. Now I'm extremely optimistic about my future, because my college education also taught me self-reliance, time management, and the value of hard work.

3. Did your family have any influence on your choice of college?

My family had several suggestions to make, but they realized I was pretty sure of myself and knew what I wanted. They stood back and let me decide. They agreed with my decision when I shared the results of my research with them.

4. What was your major in college?

I majored in _____ with a minor in _____.

5. What made you choose_____ as your major?

(Your answer here will obviously depend on your individual situation. Here are two scripted responses. The first is for people who majored in a subject or area that directly applies to their careers. The second is for those who majored in one thing and are doing another.)

I always knew _____ (business management/electrical engineering) was where I had the most potential, and I've remained with it because I turned out to be right. Not everyone is as fortunate as I have been. It's very difficult at 18 to predict and plan for the future; but, even then, I knew what I wanted to do. I'm glad I set my goals at a young age. It has worked out well for me.

OR

When I was 18, nothing in the world seemed so important as _____ (U.S. history/philosophy/English literature), and I studied for the sake of learning. Later, I realized I needed further education in subjects that would help me in my career.

6. Do you feel you made the right choice?

(Again, the first answer is for those who never made a career veer, and the second is for the rest of the world.)

Absolutely, and my career success bears me out. I am very happy with the path my life and work have followed.

OR

Yes, at the time I did. I learned a great deal, and I believe in the value of education. I, of course, went on to learn more, both formally and on the job, that applies directly to my field. I'm glad I started out in one area and switched to another. It has enhanced my ability to be creative and flexible because I have learned different approaches to performing the work successfully.

7. **How have your education and training prepared you for the job?**

My education gave me the tools to succeed, and my training taught me how to do the job properly. Before I really knew what my job entailed, I only *thought* I would perform it well.

The training gave me the opportunity to apply my education. By having the chance to do the work expected of me in advance, I gained the confidence to meet future challenges and the experience to do so successfully. The real challenge starts where the education and training end.

Studying diligently and practicing constantly really paid off. Now I am confident in my work and have earned the respect of my coworkers.

8. **What specialized training have you received to improve your job skills?**

(From the three choices given, choose one answer that most closely applies to your situation.)

After beginning my career, I saw that my _____ (high school diploma/vocational education/undergraduate degree) wasn't enough. I needed knowledge of a higher and more specific level, so I went back to school to get a _____ (bachelor/master) of _____, which I (will complete/completed) in _____ . By integrating my studies with actual job experience, I found I could leverage the value I received through my education. I estimate I learned about 10 times as much that specifically applies to this field during my _____ (graduate) work.

OR

I took every opportunity that arose to attend classes, seminars, and workshops in this area. Even when my employer wasn't sponsoring the education, I used my own money and personal time to learn what I needed to know. It really paid off.

(If you can, mention two or three well-known and reputable seminars, especially those linked to schools prominent in the field—such as Wharton, Stanford, or AMA-sponsored seminars for management candidates.)

(Finally, if no further formal education:)

I know education is important. When we stop learning, we stop growing and achieving. Since I began my career _____ years ago, I have been so thoroughly occupied with the demands of work that my ongoing education has been through on-the-job learning, company-sponsored training, and similar activities. I read everything I can find that applies to my profession, subscribe to its trade journals, and keep myself current on new developments.

9. **Why didn't you continue your formal education?**

Two reasons. The first was my impatience to earn rather than learn. The second reason was that I enjoyed being productive. As I mentioned, I worked part-time to pay my college expenses, and I was fortunate to be employed by some excellent companies.

My employers always seemed to want more of my time and talents, and in many cases, I was working at levels beyond what I was studying in my classes. Finally, I left school in my _____ year and devoted myself full-time to my career. I've never regretted that decision because I have continue to learn and grow with my work.

10. How did you do in school?

Dean's list throughout, with a _____ grade point average.

OR

Above average—mostly Bs and some Cs. I worked and was involved in many extracurricular activities while maintaining a low B/high C average.

OR

My grades were average, but I spent a great deal of time achieving in other areas, such as part-time employment and extracurricular activities like _____ (mention activities and affiliations related to the work for which you are applying). I always did my work thoroughly. As with most other people, if I could do it again, my grades probably would be much higher. I'd not only work harder, but I've learned a lot since then!

11. How did you finance your education?

I worked part-time to pay expenses and (if applicable) had a financial aid package that included scholarships and student loans.

12. Are you currently taking, or do you plan to take, any evening courses?

I am presently studying _____ at _____, which I find very valuable to my ongoing job performance and general knowledge.

OR

With the demands of keeping up with my job while interviewing, I haven't signed up for anything this semester; but as soon as I've made a decision and settled into my new position, I'm sure I'll be looking at those catalogs again. There's always something being offered that can help me perform better and bring new ideas to my work. I like to learn about new developments. Education is a lifelong process.

13. Do you subscribe to trade or professional journals? Which ones?

Yes, I subscribe to and read _____. (Mention the most influential journals in your field. If you don't know them, do some research. If you've ever contributed an article that was published, mention that as well. If you don't subscribe now, get your hands on back issues and mail in your subscription orders before you begin interviewing. It makes career sense to be conversant about new developments in your profession, no matter what your current job level.)

14. **In the past year, have you attended any professional seminars or conferences? At your own expense?**

Yes, I attended _____ in _____ (month) and (if applicable, continue listing) _____ in _____ (month). My employer paid my registration fees. I would have attended at my own expense, however, because these courses were valuable to improving my productivity.

OR

No, not in the past year, but at other times in the past I've attended seminars and workshops on _____ and _____ given by various organizations in the field. Because there are so many seminars available, it's important to be careful in making a selection. Otherwise, there would be no time left to apply what is learned.

Because I'm selective, I always get something out of every educational program I attend. If a program is offered that would help me improve my knowledge or ability in my work, I'd attend on my own time and at my own expensc.

15. What are your educational goals for the future?

My goal is to do everything possible to keep learning and improving. Things change so rapidly that we cannot rely on what we learned ten, five, even two years ago. Some of my education will be informal reading, research, and simply paying attention to what is going on. You can learn a lot just by listening to the right people and watching them.

(If applicable:)

Also, however, I _____ (am taking/plan to take) courses in _____ at _____ (name of school) and hope to complete a (bachelor of _____/ master of _____) by _____ (date).

16. Did your grade point average reflect your work ability?

My grades were above average to excellent, and I think my work record has been the same. There is a different method of evaluation in school, of course, and I've worked harder on the job than I did in school. At work, it's results that count, and I've always been able to achieve results. It's not just what you *know*, but what you *do* with what you *know*. This has always been my formula for career success.

OR

I earned average grades in school, but my work record has been good to excellent. In school you are evaluated simply by how well you *show* what you know. At work it's what you *do* with what you know—the results you achieve—that counts for everything. I've always concentrated on the result, and I've always delivered.

17. Name three things you learned in school that could be used on this job.

Many of the subjects I studied in school specifically apply to this field, including _____, _____, and _____. Yet what school really taught me that has worked throughout my career was how to solve problems, how to apply myself, and, finally, how to set a goal and achieve it.

18. What was your favorite subject in college?

(Even if the answer to this question is scuba diving or mountain climbing, try to think of a subject that will mean something to a prospective employer. Invariably, this will be something job related or business oriented.)

The turning point for me was when I took a course in _____. It opened my eyes to the possibilities in this business, and I found I had the potential to be successful at it.

19. **Did your college grades differ after military service?**

If no, then the answer is simply "No."

(If yes:)

Yes, the military changes most people, because it demands self-discipline and self-reliance. I was a good student before the military but when I returned to school after I was discharged, there was a definite improvement in my grades. No excuses, only excellence. I wouldn't settle for less. I was there to learn.

20. **Have you ever been tutored? In what subjects?**

No, I never had any particular difficulty in school.

OR

Yes, when I was in _____ (elementary/junior high/high school), I needed tutoring for a brief period in _____ (English/math). It was beneficial to have one-on-one extra help like that. It helped me overcome a temporary obstacle and gave me an even stronger foundation in those skills.

21. Why didn't you do better in school?

I guess I was just involved with other activities and growing up. I always got along with my teachers and classmates, and I even won awards for _____ (perfect attendance/science projects/debate club). The importance of grades did not have an impact on me then. Today I realize the value of formal academic achievement, and my career marks have always been well above average.

Chapter

3

Character Traits

DELIVERY

Character is the most subjective area of all. Your personality probably changed several times today *alone*.

When is your best time of day for interviewing? Are your peak hours in the morning when your mind and body are rested? Are you irritable before lunch? Lethargic after lunch? Energetic in the midafternoon? All of the above?

How about your best days of the week? Is Monday morning particularly rough for you? It is for people who are hiring. They're flooded with calls and walk-ins from weekend ads, Friday fireds, and rookie recruiters.

Unlike professional actors, interviewing pros can *schedule* the best time for themselves. You'll be surprised at how that will affect your delivery—looks, posture, attitude, reaction time, and overall confidence can dramatically improve.

What about the fuel in that walkin', talkin', interviewin', jobgettin' machine? As I said in *How to Turn an Interview into a Job*:

> I recommend coffee highly as insurance to keep you on your toes during the interview, and improve your attentiveness and attitude. Coffee has a predictable, harmless, positive effect for interviewing purposes. Caffeine is more than just a stimulant—it is an antidepressant and actually has been proven to cause the neurons in the brain to fire faster. This means you actually will store and retrieve information more rapidly.

The employer probably furnishes coffee to employees. (Don't ask, though.) There's a reason. One cup a few minutes before the interview should give you an extra edge. Too many cups will have you ready to jump over it. So experiment before the appointment.

Eat a light snack a few minutes before the interview, also. The perfect one is those peanut butter or cheese sandwich crackers. They're convenient and contain just the right amount of carbohydrates, protein, and fiber to have your incredible interviewing innards operating at peak efficiency.

So much for character traits.

SCRIPT

1. Do you consider yourself to be a smart person?

Yes. That means I'm smart enough to know my opinion is biased. The kind of intelligence required on the job isn't always measured by an IQ test. Only through coping with different situations and interacting with other people can intelligence truly be judged. By these criteria, I'm above average in intelligence.

When it comes to working with people, solving business problems, and making decisions—especially those related to the job—I'm as good as or better than anyone else. There are many things I don't know, but I can learn. In that way, a smart person is one who asks questions, listens carefully, and realizes nobody knows everything.

2. How important is job security to you?

Security is a basic need, but I know that there are no guarantees in life. The only true job security comes from making a meaningful contribution to my employer. If I know my job will be around for as long as I excel at it, I am able to concentrate on my work and remain focused. The best environment is one where employer and employee form a partnership for their mutual benefit.

The first priority of any job is the work itself. Everything else is secondary. As long as I am challenged by my work and respected by those around me, I'm confident that I'll be able to continue getting the work done properly, always meeting or exceeding expectations.

3. Do you get bored doing the same work over and over again?

Not really. If the work involves my job, I don't get bored because it is my responsibility to complete it to the best of my ability. Work is not necessarily entertaining; it is something that must be routinely and successfully accomplished time after time. That's why they call it "work" and why I am being paid to do it.

If someone gets bored with repetition, he or she might have a serious problem. Sometimes you just have to set your preferences aside and focus on what needs to be done—even if it isn't something new.

I guess I've always been too busy doing my job to get bored.

4. Do you prefer working as a member of a team or would you rather work alone?

Working as part of a team is one of the most important elements in a successful career and life. If you can't work well on a team, you probably can't work and communicate well on a one-on-one basis either.

While teamwork is very important, I can work just as hard alone. Though more pressure to produce might exist, it would also prove to be a challenge. Whether I prefer to work as part of a team or alone depends on the best way to complete the job. Either way, I would work equally hard with the initiative required for success.

5. What are the reasons for your success?

I always give 100 percent. Some people try to prove themselves to someone else, but I think sometimes it's better to prove to yourself that you can succeed. No one is a better judge of your success than you, and you know what you can do. When I do a job well, it gives me personal satisfaction that carries over into everything I do.

Working very hard does not prevent me from getting along with all sorts of people. By respecting everyone as an individual as you advance in responsibility, you not only make a good impression, but also you gain the respect of others.

Paying attention to details is also important. I usually like to recheck everything I do, just in case I missed something the first time. I also find it beneficial to at least review my work that has my name on it, even if completed by a secretary or someone else in my department. Proper delegation requires some supervision.

Eventually, hard work, respect for others, and attention to detail pay off, and they make the job more enjoyable and challenging along the way.

6. Do you like to work with "things"?

(If yes, or if the job requires manual/technical aptitude:)

Yes, I've always had an aptitude for the absolute and definable. I have good technical ability and can make things work. I have the ability, however, to conceptualize a job and then translate those concepts into reality.

(If no, or if the job is more abstract:)

Yes, but usually as the result of design and concept. This work takes ideas, imagination, and the ability to formulate a project from beginning to end—see it first, then specify what it will take for others to make it work. I'm the idea person, but I pride myself on being a practical realist. An idea is only as good as its use.

7. Do you like to work with facts and figures?

(If yes, or if the job requires analytical and math skills:)

Absolutely. That's the basis of this work. I've always had a flair for the numbers side of the business, and my thought processes are very analytical and precise. Accurate books and records are an essential management tool and can help to identify areas that need improvement.

(If no, or if the job likely would not fit the thinker/ analyzer personality:)

Facts and figures are important. I respect them, I'm good with them, but I don't get bogged down in them. I always read the reports, and I'm quick to spot inconsistencies and errors. I don't check *every* number twice, though, because that's not what produces *results*. Financial records are like X rays that allow a doctor to make a diagnosis. I leave the preparation to the skilled technicians.

8. Do you like to work with people?

(If yes, or if it's a teamwork situation:)

Without a doubt. If we're to meet our goals and keep up with the growth that's predicted for this industry, we'll have to organize and coordinate the efforts of many people. There's a *synergy* in teamwork that can accomplish far more than the same individuals could working alone. When people work together, there's nothing like it. The energy and creativity they activate in each other are many times greater—the whole is greater than the sum of its parts.

(If the job requires solitary hours analyzing reports or crunching numbers:)

I've always worked well with others, but I have no difficulty getting my work done independently. I'm a self-starter. I can set my goals, or I can take assigned goals and complete them. I'm comfortable with myself.

9. Are you absent from work often?

(If your work record shows extended absence as the result of an injury or illness that is no longer a factor, explain what happened and why it no longer affects your attendance. Otherwise, use the following:)

No, my attendance record is very good. I think you'll see when you check that the few days I missed work were due to the usual flu viruses going around. I figure, when you're sick, it's better to take one day off and get well rather than going to the office, working at half speed, and taking more time off to recuperate. I'd rather work at home when I'm sick than expose coworkers to my illness.

I'm in good health and rebound quickly. I've noticed that people who miss a lot of work really don't like their jobs or themselves very well.

10. Do you get bored with detail?

No. I'm getting paid to do what the job requires. If checking details is part of what it takes to do the job right, then that's what I do. Success and advancement are not boring, and they directly result from doing your work well.

11. How do you show your interest in your co-workers?

By keeping my eyes and ears open. I try to be sensitive to those around me. If someone behaves in a way that is different from what I expect, I ask myself, "Why? Are there problems that have caused this person to perform differently?"

On a day-to-day basis, I try to remember the little things that are important to the people around me. I follow up and ask them how things are going without becoming overbearing. Work teams often become like a family, and it's important to remember that coworkers need to be appreciated, liked, and respected.

If I am the supervisor in the relationship, I usually call a quick, closed-door conference to see if there's something that can be done before a possible problem becomes a probable one.

12. If you could be anyone, whom would you like to be?

(Now, here's a chance to really get "unhired" if you're not careful. Use the answer I've given or modify it to adapt it to your own personality, but don't reveal a fantasy that's too fantastic. Remember, you're in an interviewer's office, not on your psychotherapist's couch.)

Generally, I'd say I'm pretty happy with who I am and what I have done with my life. If I could be anything or anyone I wanted, it would be a person who used (his/her) business skills to make the world a better place. There's a great law of life that I try to live: The best way to succeed is by helping others to succeed.

13. What career or business would you consider if you were starting over again?

I like what I'm doing now. I chose it, and it has worked out well for me. I suppose the only other work I would consider is _____.

(At this point, mention something related to the target job. For example, if the company manufactures hospital products, you might say, ". . . being a health-care professional, because my work in this field has shown me that the work we are doing is important and that I do it well." This is a direct, upbeat, high-scoring answer.

You would also be safe mentioning a field related to an outside activity you enjoy, one that demonstrates other skills the employer might be able to use, for example:)

Although I'm well suited to _____ (accounting/general management/operations), I like to design and build things. I've remodeled our kitchen and built a sunroom addition as well as play equipment for my kids. I've often thought I might have gone into architecture or drafting and design if I hadn't gone to business school. If I had, I'd probably be running a business on the side!

(Another example, if applicable:)

I might have become a journalist or writer. I've had the opportunity to contribute articles and comments to _____ and _____ (names of professional journals), and I enjoy the discipline of researching a topic and communicating it clearly. My ability to conceptualize an article—as well as to research, write, and revise it—really facilitates the written communication required in this work.

14. How do you react to criticism by superiors if you believe it is unwarranted?

Criticism is never unwarranted, but it is often *unwelcome*. No one likes to be criticized, and many people are insulted. When they're hurt or angry, they either overreact or block out the criticism entirely. Even unnecessary criticism is *caused* by something. If it was something I did, I want to know as soon as possible so I can clarify the misunderstanding.

I've learned to think about the other person's comments for a while, so I can see them as feedback to my *actions*, not rejection of *me*. Why did the other individual see what I did as negative?

Once I've taken time to think, I can respond, rather than merely react. If I still feel the criticism was unjust or was the result of some misunderstanding, I schedule a few minutes to sit down and talk it over calmly with my manager. I always try to present my case with a smile on my face and without placing blame.

I have learned that being right isn't always the best thing, especially if you're telling someone else that he or she is wrong. It might feel good at first to get someone else to back down, but usually it doesn't do much for the long-term working relationship. The important thing is to place the derailed train back on the track so it will start moving again. When work is going along smoothly, it doesn't matter who is right and who is *wrong*. It matters that you're all part of a successful effort and that you all share in the rewards of that success. That train can be an express if everyone works together.

15. Do you have any fear that might deter you from traveling by air?

(If you have an enduring phobia that prevents you from traveling by air, you shouldn't be applying for an astronaut's job. Go for what you know and like.)

None at all. I've always recognized that the speed of air travel is necessary to business, and I've traveled routinely in past jobs. The most important thing is to get in front of the customer so I can make the sale (solve the problem), and I view it as all in a day's (or night's) work.

16. What would you do if it were your last day on earth?

That's a tough question, but not as tough as having it happen! I'd gather the people who are important to me and really let them know how much they've contributed to my happiness. I've led a fulfilling life and enjoy what I do every day. The book can close on anyone at any time. That's why it's important to live it a page at a time.

17. Would you be willing to take a lie detector test?

Yes, I have nothing to hide and always make it a practice to tell the truth. But, if taking a lie detector test is a requirement of employment here, I'd like to know the purpose and accuracy of the test.

18. Name three books you've read in the past six months.

(Your secret's safe with me! Keep your eye on the business bestseller list and mention three current titles. Management-oriented ones give you the highest marks.)

19. Do you have a competitive nature?

Yes. A competitive nature is necessary to be successful in a corporate environment. But competitiveness doesn't mean vying with my coworkers for recognition, raises, or promotions. If I do my work well and always give my best effort, the rewards will come. I've found that's the only real way to succeed.

But I do compete with myself. I'm always trying to break my own record—to do something better or faster than I did it the last time. I'm especially competitive when it comes to improving my company's product or service.

There's so much potential for accomplishment when you're part of a vibrant company like this one.

20. What is your idea of success?

To wake up in the morning and feel good about what I will achieve during the day, to meet each new challenge with confidence in my ability, and to have the respect of my fellow employees.

If I am successful, I will continue to be given new challenges that develop my abilities and make me even more productive. Having fulfilling work to do, doing it well, and participating with others in reaching our goals—that's my idea of success.

21. How would you feel about working for a female executive?

I'm an equal opportunity employee. I enjoy working for anyone who practices good management and knows how to tap the potential of team members. Talent has no gender.

22. What would you like inscribed on your headstone?

I hope you're not taking orders! I'm just not ready to go yet. Life's too enjoyable, and I have a lot more to accomplish before my days are over.

I hope it can say: "(He/She) was a good person, lived a useful life, helped and respected others, and left the world a better place than when (he/she) entered it."

23. What types of people try your patience?

Well, patience goes a long way in understanding why people do things that cause others to react negatively. I try to save my reaction until I've explored the reasons.

The only kind of people who try my patience are those who intentionally and repeatedly don't do their jobs properly. If you've accepted a job and the paycheck that goes with it, you owe it to the employer and the customer to do your best.

24. How well do you cope with tension?

I've adopted several techniques. There is so much available on the subject, so I've developed a program that works well for me. I eat properly, exercise regularly, and take vitamins. When work causes tension for whatever reason—deadlines, schedules, special projects, and unexpected obstacles—I'm ready.

Also, I try to keep a perspective on the situation. There's nothing you can't accomplish if you set your mind to it. History has proven that. *My* history, too. We've all had to turn mountains into stepping stones. Eventually, as one success spawns another, those mountains start to look smaller. They're not—it's just that self-confidence and experience make *you* bigger. I realize no stressful situation lasts forever, so I just set my sights high and keep climbing without looking down. I've already been there. Climbing is so much more fun when you realize what awaits you at the top.

25. Do you speak up if your point of view differs from that of your superiors?

I'm not a yes person, but I am careful about *how* I express my opinions. I don't disagree vehemently with my superiors or coworkers in front of others. During staff meetings I take notes, formulate my ideas fully, and then present them to the other person privately. You can disagree without being disagreeable. In fact, it's much more likely your opinion will be accepted—and appreciated.

People don't like to be nailed in front of others, and it's a waste of time and energy to cause unnecessary dissent on the job. Private meetings and carefully worded memos that aren't distributed to the entire organization get the message across much more effectively. Few points are worth making at the expense of morale.

How you say something determines whether your opinions will be heard or not. Instead of opening with a statement like, "I don't agree with you on the subject of delegation," I might say, "I've been reviewing methods of delegation and have an idea about how we can drive up our efficiency measurably. Would you like to hear it?"

26. Are you an innovative person?

It appears that way. Innovation shows up in small ways, as well as large. While I haven't redesigned an entire product line, I *have* made improvements wherever I've worked over the years. They resulted in saving time and money and were a more sensible alternative to the way things were done previously. Sometimes, innovation is just the application of common sense. That's why most inventions seem so simple after they're developed!

I also can work well with the company's creative staff, communicating my ideas to them so they can use their talent to produce something tangible. In this way, I've contributed to the creation of and the innovation in many projects.

27. How often do you lose your temper?

Rarely. However, it's a good thing to lose—permanently. I've never lost my temper at work. At best, it's a waste of time and energy. At worst, it makes people un-comfortable and diminishes your effectiveness.

Even if you're completely right about something, losing your temper often destroys your ability to con-vince others that you are right. Venting anger is inappro-priate in a business, team-oriented environment.

28. How have you benefited from your disappointments?

I'm glad you said "disappointments" rather than "failures" because no one fails until he or she stops try-ing. Every disappointment is a learning experience, and one you would not have had otherwise. Each time one has occurred, whether in my work or personal life, I've been able to tell myself, "Okay, so now I know not to do *that*." Through trial and error, a conscientious person eventually learns what works.

My biggest disappointments have been the ones I've tried hardest to overcome. It's worked pretty well because I have fewer and fewer disappointments as the years go by.

29. How confident are you about addressing a trade group or seminar audience?

(If you feel comfortable and have experience with public speaking:)

Even though I've had speech classes and extra training in presentation techniques, I used to be nervous about speaking in front of groups. Yet I found that preparation, practice, and knowing my subject helped me overcome this. I've also found that the world won't wobble on its axis if I admit I don't know something. An audience can sense when you're bluffing—what you *convey* overpowers what you *say*.

Now, within the first few minutes, I'm consistently able to develop rapport with my audience, and it's no different from talking to you like I'm doing now. I know my material and present it in a logical, organized, and interesting manner. When people accept the messenger, they accept the message. That's what teaching is all about.

(If you're not comfortable with public speaking, but know the job requires it:)

I am comfortable presenting my material in an informal setting, such as this meeting, or to a smaller group, like a staff meeting. However, extemporaneous speaking is an essential communication skill. I'd welcome the opportunity to learn more about how to present ideas effectively.

30. Can you name three of your biases?

Let's see, three of them. Well, first, I tend to be biased *against* people who intentionally don't perform their jobs to the best of their abilities, who think they are doing the employer a favor by being there.

Second, I'm biased *in favor of* getting the work done when I promised and how I promised. I guess you could call it a sense of commitment; and I expect that same level of commitment from coworkers.

Finally, I tend to be biased *in favor of* an organization that fosters challenge and increased responsibility.

31. Do you feel the only way to get a job done right is to do it yourself?

No, that kind of attitude results in mismanagement. If I am the only person in my group with a particular skill, my first priority after completing the task is to train someone else to do it in my absence.

Effective team management requires that the job gets done even when some of the players are on the road, at a meeting, or on assignment elsewhere. I don't delegate responsibility and then forget about it, however. If I have ultimate responsibility for something, I follow up to make sure it is done. I'm a pilot, but I believe in a trained copilot—and then in an automatic pilot, properly programmed, to keep us flying right on course.

32. If you could do anything, what would you do?

I'd keep on doing what I'm doing now. I have meaningful work with daily challenges and rewards. I don't have any desire for an easy life. That's a contradiction in terms—nothing worth having in life comes easily. For now, I'm interested in achievement, accomplishment, and seeing just how much I can do with the talent and intelligence I have.

33. Do you get along with your coworkers?

Yes, I do. Good working relationships are essential to a successful career and to getting the work done, so I have always tried to foster them. But there's a definite difference between being friendly with your coworkers and working with friends.

It's important to maintain just enough distance to be able to deal with problems that arise without being hampered by personal feelings. Professional detachment is directly related to objectivity and, therefore, effectiveness.

34. What can you tell me about yourself?

I'm a self-starter, highly motivated, energetic, and results oriented, but cooperative and a team player as well. I'm a good communicator and can help others focus on a goal and motivate them to attain it.

Enthusiasm and energy are contagious, and I'm infected with both. As a result, the groups I've worked with become highly charged and very successful.

I'm persuasive, but I also have good listening skills.

I'm sensitive to my environment and those around me. I value excellence.

35. What do you think you do best?

(Mention your specific job talents and skills that are applicable to the target job and employer. Write them in the lines provided and rehearse them. Then conclude with the high-scoring final paragraph.)

_____

_____

_____

_____

_____

In addition, I am adaptable and flexible. There is rarely only one right answer. I can call on my past experience and apply it to the problem at hand. I can teach myself new skills and have a proven ability to transfer my job skills to new areas successfully.

36. What have you learned from your mistakes?

Almost everything I've learned! If you never made a mistake, you'd probably never learn anything new. Someone who doesn't make mistakes doesn't take risks. Sometimes you must risk to grow, and all risks can result in mistakes. When I've made a mistake, I've acknowledged the error but used it as a lesson to keep me from making the same mistake again. It's all part of the educational process, of growth.

However, I weigh potential outcomes carefully before deciding on a course of action. In this way, I measure the risks against the use of my employer's resources. Making a mistake is inevitable, but not anticipating it is inexcusable.

We all make mistakes. It is what we do with the lessons learned from our mistakes that determines our success in life.

37. Do you work well under pressure?

Definitely. Positive pressure can be the tightly coiled spring that forces the release of untapped reserves of energy and initiative. Some of the greatest events in history were the result of pressure situations, when someone was called on to make a quick decision and act on that decision. Positive pressure brings out the best in people.

However, when pressure, tension, and emergencies become the daily routine in any organization, positive pressure becomes a negative. Resources are used up and people burn out. A competent manager knows how to control the pressure and dispense it in effective doses.

38. What are your feelings about a large company?

I welcome the opportunity to work in a large, developed, well-known organization such as this. The resources and potential for advancement in a large organization are not available in smaller companies. I'd be proud to add my skills and abilities to the excellence that flourishes here.

39. What are your feelings about a medium-sized company?

Medium-sized companies have emerged from their growing pains and are more secure in their markets than smaller companies. Yet, they haven't become large and impersonal. They are still able to respond quickly to change and accept the individuality that fosters innovation. This gives employees a sense of not being too far removed from the decision-making processes. I like the potential for being involved in even more growth with a company this size.

40. What are your feelings about a small company?

The advantage of working in a company of this size is getting in on the ground floor of something that is happening, helping it meet its challenges, and participating as it thrives and prospers. There's a hands-on involvement that brings a sense of accomplishment not available in a larger, more established organization. From what I have seen and heard, this company is going places, and I'd like to travel with it to the top.

41. Wouldn't you be better off in another company?

No, I'm sure I wouldn't. The type of opportunity and challenge I seek are here. Furthermore, my skills and experience match what *you're* looking for. I've researched my options thoroughly, and this company comes out on top for me. That's why I'm here.

42. Do you consider yourself aggressive?

I think the word I'd use to describe myself would be *assertive* rather than *aggressive*. When I think of an aggressive person, I think of someone who bullies or steamrolls others to get his or her way. Being assertive, on the other hand, allows me to make my ideas known without disparaging the ideas and opinions of others. It allows for a mutually fulfilling, two-way exchange, without anyone's being put down or attacked.

43. What do other people think of the way you work?

The formal feedback from my superiors on my performance reviews has always been positive. Informally, I've been praised by fellow employees as well. I've made it a goal to earn the respect of coworkers, and I've been successful in achieving that goal.

44. Describe the perfect job.

The perfect job is one that offers daily challenges, provides the kind of stimulation that keeps my skills and abilities at peak levels, and allows me to achieve tangible results on a regular basis—something that is fast paced without being frantic, in a situation where new ideas and creativity are fostered.

The perfect job is in an organization that's progressive and competitive. I want to be a part of a winning team and to make a significant contribution to its success.

45. What public figures are your role models? Why?

(In answering this question, it's all right to give specific names of individuals, as long as you are careful to avoid those who are controversial. You'll be encountering the interviewer's own biases in this matter, and you don't know what they are. Rather than choose partisan political figures, you should mention the names of neutral individuals, such as highly regarded leaders in your community, well-known academic figures, or historical household names.)

I admire anyone who has the courage of his or her convictions and is not afraid to express them, like _____. People like _____, who do something with their lives and contribute to society are also high on my list. Finally, those with new ideas, the innovators in science and the arts, such as _____, are people I admire.

46. Name five things that motivate you.

One, daily challenges.

Two, tangible results.

Three, understanding and assisting to achieve my employer's goals.

Four, the opportunity to work as part of a talented team of individuals.

Five, respect for a job well done and encouragement to use creativity and initiative in finding new ways to do things.

47. What would you like to be remembered for?

For accepting new challenges and being equal to them. For always being willing to go the extra mile, work the extra hour, and give what was needed to get the job done. For getting the job done with a minimum of complaints. For encouraging others in the company to give their best.

48. Tell me a story.

Once upon a time there was a (man/woman) who heard about a great company to work for, called

_____. So (he/she) did some investigating and found that the good things were true, that the company hired creative, self-motivated professionals and gave them the opportunity to shine, both individually and as part of a dynamic team. (He/She) also found that the company expected excellence from its employees.

(He/She) saw that (his/her) skills and abilities matched the company's needs, so (he/she) completed an application, attached (his/her) resume, sent it to the company's (human resources director/personnel manager), and obtained an interview. The interview went very well, and the (man/woman) was even more enthusiastic about the possibilities for (his/her) career growth at this company. To be continued . . .

49. How would a friend describe you?

Likeable, energetic, and an organizer who is always thinking of different ways to make being with friends fulfilling and enjoyable. Someone who keeps personal commitments, protects personal confidences, and makes the time to help the community. A family person whose house is in order.

50. Would you prefer to work with numbers or words?

(If you are applying for a position that requires strength in a specific area, you should emphasize your particular abilities and how they apply to the target job. The first answer below is a neutral answer, the second answer is for numbers-oriented professions, and the third is for jobs that require special communications skills. Choose one for your script.)

Actually, I like both. I'm a good communicator, and language skills—written and verbal—have always come easily to me. At the same time, I enjoy numerical analysis and number crunching. I appreciate a job that requires the use of both talents because diversity in my work allows me to change gears, get something else done, and then come back to the first task with a fresh approach.

OR

While I am skilled at both, this work requires an exceptional grasp of numbers and the statistical side of business, which has always been a strength of mine.

Statistical reports logically tell you about financial strengths and weaknesses. The numbers don't lie. As you can see from my resume, I have a great deal of experience in gathering, analyzing, and interpreting statistical data.

OR

While I have a good head for figures, as they say, my main strength is in communications, both written and oral. I'm a creative and expressive writer and an organized and fluent speaker. Both of those skills are essential to success in this business. I know how to use numbers to arrive at a conclusion and support my decisions, however.

51. Do you think you can get along with _____?

(This is a loaded question. When it is asked by an interviewer, he or she usually has someone specific in mind. Often, it's a company president or other top manager whose personality is rigid and everyone else in the organization must learn to adapt to it. A common variation is, "Do you think you can get along with a very dictatorial, strong-willed individual?" Your reply should be:)

I have always found that people admire in others the traits they like about themselves. Someone with a strong will is very likely proud of that strong will and doesn't mind when others show conviction. Sometimes you can be of greatest assistance by speaking your mind candidly but carefully.

In the past, I've always been conscious of my position and acted accordingly. I don't let the personalities of others affect how I feel about them. I judge them by the quality and quantity of their work. I get along with anyone whose accomplishments I can respect.

There's a saying: "Everyone looks strange to someone else." When it comes to accepting others, that says it all.

52. Will you be able to cope with a change in work environment after working ____ years in your last job?

Definitely, I welcome the challenge of learning about and adapting to a new environment. That's one of the reasons I'm seeking to make a change right now. Any organization benefits from new blood, and I'd like to transfer all I've experienced to this company, while at the same time having the opportunity to meet new challenges and achieve new goals.

53. How do you feel about company policy?

Policies are an essential part of any business. Some structure is necessary. It helps people make decisions and gives them a sense of direction. I've always followed company policy and have been instrumental in translating it into understandable, workable procedures.

54. Are you a self-starter?

Yes, I am. I have the ability to see what needs to be done and the resources to do it. I can set expectations for my work that are usually higher than others set for me, and I can achieve them. I'm a quick study and can be up and running with a minimum of instruction and training.

55. **Would you work if you did not need money
to support yourself?**

Yes, I would. Having something meaningful to do—
a reason to wake up in the morning, problems to solve,
and goals to accomplish—is what life is about to me. I
feel much better in a business suit than a leisure suit.

I suppose a life of leisure would be nice for a while;
and, if I acquired a fortune, I might try it—for a month or
two. But, then I would get restless. Because there's not
much chance I'll ever be independently wealthy, my career remains my first priority.

56. **Are you sensitive to constructive criticism?**

Not at all. *Constructive* is the key word in that
question. It is important to see criticism as useful feedback on what we've done, not who we are. Managers, or
any individuals, who have learned to criticize construc-
tively can help others realize much more of their potential than if no one ever gave them the benefit of such
insight.

57. **Do you have an analytical mind?**

In the sense that I can identify problems and work
out solutions to them, yes. I have above average ana-

lytical skills. Like anything else, good analytical skills come through practice, through using that amazing computer between your ears on a regular basis. That's why I'm looking for work that requires me to think *and* act.

58. Are you interested in research?

I'm always interested in new developments that will make operations more efficient or improve the product. When we stop discovering, learning, and creating, we cease to exist—as an industry and as a civilization. I welcome any job assignment that would call on me to further the research in this field.

59. Do you arrive at work on time?

Yes. If I have a problem being on time—due to car trouble, for example—I always call and explain the situation. Also, I'm very diligent in making up any time I've missed due to an emergency.

More than obeying a clock, I look on work and my job as an assignment that must be done and done well. If the work I'm required to do in a day is not done, my day is not over. I either stay to complete it or take it home. The next day's work awaits when I arrive in the morning.

60. What is the most foolish thing you've ever done?

I suppose we've all had our foolish moments. Mine were mostly the result of youthful free-spiritedness. I'm fortunate that nothing I did had any negative or long-lasting consequences.

When it comes to my career, I'm pleased there's no foolishness to report. Every step has been carefully planned and executed to give both me and my employer maximum benefit. Although there have been a few mistakes and disappointments, I was quick to learn from them so I didn't repeat them.

Chapter

4

Initiative and Creativity

DELIVERY

Have you ever noticed how much initiative you have when you're uncomfortable? You're also highly creative in devising ways to bring yourself back into your comfort zone. The more you itch, the more you scratch.

For interviewing purposes, concentrate on the parts of former jobs that you improved. Then work backwards—if "necessity is the mother of invention," then "invention is the daughter of necessity." Focus on *what* you did, then *why*.

Next, tie these improvements into the target job. You'll be surprised how easy this is, because initiative and creativity are highly transferable. Once you learn how to scratch, it doesn't matter where you itch.

Scratch out your script using the following questions as a guide.

SCRIPT

1. What do you do when you have trouble solving a problem?

One thing I *don't* do is ignore it and hope it will go away. I'm not afraid to ask questions or to look for the answers myself. There is a solution to every problem. Sometimes, it just takes creative investigation. I'm a problem solver by nature. Nothing puzzles me for long—if it does, I just keep working until I find the solution.

2. **What have you done in your present job to make it more effective or more challenging?**

I've made my job more effective by finding ways to streamline the paperwork and administration so I can focus more effort and energy on producing *results*. Working smarter *and* harder really accomplishes a lot.

More challenging? I'm always looking for new opportunities, and I've been particularly successful in finding different applications for the existing product and its users. I _____

_____.

(Mention briefly an example of using initiative and creativity to help the company, such as "found a new market for the XYZ product among _____," or "saw a problem with the computer system and recommended _____," or something similar.)

3. **What is the most boring job you've ever had? How did you do at it?**

I haven't found any of my work in my adult career boring. I've always been to busy to be bored!

Perhaps, as a teenager, you could say I wasn't very excited about some of the part-time work available. But I always found something positive about every job. When I was behind the counter at a fast-food store selling a thousand hamburgers a day, the routine was eased by the hundreds of people I met. There has been something interesting, something that held my attention, about every job I've held, or I don't think I would have taken the job in the first place.

4. **What is the most interesting job you've ever had? How did you do at it?**

My most interesting job to date has been _____ _____ because of _____. I received particularly favorable performance reviews in that job, but I've had excellent ratings in all my work. When I make a commitment to a job, I give it all I've got.

5. **Is there a lot of pressure in your current job? How do you cope with it?**

There is pressure in every job. In my present job, the pressure is usually associated with production deadlines or special projects. Experience has taught me how to cope with pressure.

All jobs have more demands at some times than others. The key is to manage your time and prioritize the work so you're ready for anything. When I work out the details and set the schedule in advance, I see that any big job can be broken down into many smaller jobs. When taken one task at a time, any job can be mastered.

I *respond* to pressure, I don't *react* to it. After analyzing the components of a project, I take a few steps back so I can see the big picture. This approach has seen me through many a tough situation with results that exceeded what anyone imagined—except perhaps me.

6. **What do you think it takes for a person to be successful in _____ (specialty of position being discussed, such as engineering, parts assembly, customer service)?**

> I think you need good skills in _____ _____ (conceptualizing a design/working with your hands/dealing with people).
> In addition, being successful in this work requires a drive to do your best and to continually improve on your past performance. One reason I think I've succeeded is that my past accomplishments have given me self-confidence. I view each day and each task as a new challenge and an opportunity for improvement on whatever I did yesterday. Knowing that yesterday was successful helps me approach today and tomorrow with a can-do attitude. After all, I *did* do!

7. **If you encountered this situation, how would you handle it? (Typical employment situation, such as: "Your manager is out of town and cannot be reached. Only the manager has the**

authority to approve shipments over a certain value to new customers on credit. A customer you've been trying to get calls with a large order and insists that it be shipped immediately, on a *credit* basis. You know your manager wanted you to get this customer, but you don't have authorization to release the merchandise without payment. What do you do?")

I've been in a similar situation in the past. I like a big order as much as anyone else, but I also know there is a good reason for the company credit policy. When you send $10,000 worth of merchandise out the door to a new customer without payment or prior credit approval, you deserve whatever you get—or *don't* get. Most customers are accustomed to COD shipments on initial orders or to those waiting for credit approval. When customers try to circumvent these policies, it's a signal to proceed with caution or even stop.

I would call the customer back, thank him or her for the order, and let the person know how happy we are to have the business. I would explain the policy clearly and politely and offer the opportunity either to accept a COD shipment or to wait until credit is approved. I'd assure him or her I would personally expedite the paperwork and ship the order the fastest way possible once good credit was verified.

If the customer has called with an order, he or she already likes the product and price. So my job now is to deliver flawless customer service and sales follow-up. If the person is trying to put one over on me and I stand firmly and politely behind our company policy, he or she gains a new respect for the company. I have an excellent chance of keeping the business by demonstrating this kind of professionalism. That's the reason for company policies and procedures in the first place—to help employees solve problems like this on their own with firm, fair, and consistent guidelines.

8. How do you go about making important decisions?

I evaluate my options, laying them all out in front of me. I find it helps to write down briefly what my alternatives arc, so I can examine them objectively. Then I rely on past experience, company policies, and—in part—intuition to guide me to a decision. I look at each situation individually and weigh possible outcomes before making a choice.

If it is a big decision that has no precedent, I get input from those who will be affected by it—the staff—as well as those who will be called upon to explain my decision—my superiors.

9. Has anyone in the business world been an inspiration to you?

Yes, several people. I've been fortunate to work with bright, talented, energetic individuals. Several of my managers have served as informal mentors who helped me develop my own management skills and style.

In every field, the trainees learn from the pros. I've never been so sure of my abilities that I wasn't willing to listen and learn from those who had more experience and had accomplished more. I think I've learned an even greater amount from these individuals than from the textbooks I've read and the courses I've taken.

10. Are you able to work alone without direct supervision?

Definitely. I'm a self-starter *and* finisher. I usually only need direction once—the first time I do something—and, from then on, I work well on my own. I'm inner-directed and enjoy applying my creativity and problem-solving skills to my work.

However, I'm not one of those individuals who will keep doing something wrong rather than getting help, operating out of some fear of looking bad. If I'm not sure about a task or about whether I'm getting the expected results, I check with the person in charge to make sure. I'm not afraid to ask questions.

I don't believe in that old saying, "'Tis better to remain silent and be thought a fool than to open your mouth and remove any doubt." I much prefer, "It doesn't matter *who* is right, but *what* is right." The important thing is to do the job right and with the greatest efficiency and productivity.

11. How did you handle the toughest decision you ever had to make?

I remember it well. I had to _____ _____ (make a decision that would affect the jobs of several employees, perhaps require permanent lay-offs). I thought seriously about the consequences to the employer, without ignoring the human factors involved. I arrived at a solution that produced the best result for the company while minimizing the effects on the employees.

We kept the most qualified people, but those who had to leave were good employees also. We were able to help each one of them get work in the same field within a month of leaving our company. That minimized our unemployment insurance burden and kept those who were affected by the downsizing from losing self-esteem.

Making the right decision required a lot of fore-thought and looking at best- and worst-case scenarios extensively before making my recommendations. I firmly believe you have to look carefully at both the business *and* the people side of every work decision.

CHAPTER

5

Management Ability

DELIVERY

Because the ability to manage depends on sustained personal interaction with subordinates, it's virtually impossible for your skill to be measured. Interviews aren't held with understudies present.

The closest an interviewer can get is to find out whether you've learned how to apply basic principles. Asking you about results is about as reliable as asking an actor whether he or she deserves an Oscar.

What if you've never managed anyone? Not to worry. Just sensitize yourself to situations where you *supervised* others. It doesn't have to be a cast of thousands. Be ready to discuss how you helped organize those you supervised to accomplish specific tasks.

If the supervisory situations aren't job related, aim for anything that's *business* related. Even charity fund raising and community service projects can be effectively woven into the script. Managing a dozen volunteers can be the equivalent of directing a cast of hundreds earning union scale.

Your local public library stocks many books and periodicals on management. A few current ones are all you need to pick up new theories, the latest buzzwords, or an interesting case study.

Then customize your script so you sound like an M.B.A. In fact you *are*—a Most Believable Applicant!

SCRIPT

1. As a department manager, how would you go about establishing rapport with your staff?

I would first want to know as much about each individual as I could, professionally as well as personally. Every employee is an individual and cannot be evaluated solely by arbitrary standards. Independent judgment is the major part of every manager's job, and there can be several right ways to approach something.

By reviewing each individual's position and work record, I would gain insight about his or her strong points and weaknesses. Similarly, by meeting with each person on a one-to-one basis and making myself open to candid dialogue, the stage would be set for a healthy working relationship.

Too many supervisor/subordinate relationships are like two monologues rather than one dialogue. This is a management problem and a manager's responsibility to solve. In a word, I'd start by listening.

2. What makes the best manager?

The best manager is a person who is dedicated to company goals yet sensitive to the individuality of each employee he or she manages. Managing people effectively is a difficult job, but the rewards in helping them develop while contributing to company objectives are great.

Essentially, good management requires understanding human nature so people can be motivated to fulfill their potential. The best manager develops people to their fullest. He or she creates a system that allows the department to operate so efficiently that the work won't skip a beat if he or she isn't there and that also allows for smooth succession if he or she is promoted.

Exciting and igniting people is the manager's vision.

3. What do your subordinates think are your strengths?

The people who have worked for me will tell you that I am fair and that I have a balanced approach to managing, one that considers both the business and people side of every issue. They know I don't make hasty decisions that everyone will repent at leisure. And working for me usually means being on a winning team with a coach who expects everyone to give 110 percent. I ask a lot, but they love it.

4. What do your subordinates think are your weaknesses?

What might be perceived by some as weaknesses are really my strengths. I expect a lot from my staff, but no more than I expect from myself. I look for and reward people who show initiative and creativity.

People I've supervised in the past will tell you that they worked harder in my department than in any other job. They'll also tell you they enjoyed it more, because they were accomplishing more.

5. Have you ever been in a position to hire employees?

(If yes:)

Yes, making employment decisions has been a routine part of several of my past jobs and my current job as well. I have always valued the opportunity to have a say in staffing my own department. As you well know, hiring people is a real judgment call, and eventually you develop an insight—even an intuition—about who will work out and who won't. Personnel decisions are people decisions, and everyone is unique. Hiring them properly isn't really a science. It's an art—just like motivating and managing them.

(If no, but if you have related experience:)

I have never been directly responsible for hiring, but in many cases I have been asked to speak to prospective employees and later give my opinion. My superiors valued my insight and my knowledge of the job requirements in making their selection. In that way, I've indirectly hired some of my best coworkers.

6. **Tell me about the people you hired in your (current/previous) job. How long did they stay with you? How did they work out?**

I've developed a sense of the type of employee who will do a particular job well, and also a sense of which people work best together in a given situation; so there's always been a minimum of unrest and turnover among the troops.

I think any manager's best bet is to be candid right from the start. I don't overstate or oversell the job, but I let prospective employees know we value their contributions. I also let them know what I expect and what the job entails. It's important to get the right person for the job, or both the person and the job suffer.

Once you hire people, you must take the time to train them properly and give them the tools they need to do the job right. Then you determine who will work best with a minimum of guidance and who needs more supervision. Management is like a dance for which you anticipate the music to stay in step. It doesn't have to cause corporate musical chairs.

7. **What are some of the things your (current/previous) employer might have done to be more successful?**

I don't overanalyze the reasons for management decisions. Any decision is only as good as the facts on which it is based. Management has access to market research, projections, and other important data. Yet, sometimes, even with the best input, things don't work out. Overall, the companies I've worked for have been very sound, and I learned a great deal from the successes *and* their failures. In fact, the failures can be the *reasons* for the successes!

8. In what manner do you communicate with staff? With superiors?

In most cases, a manager must develop a uniform and consistent communication style so that employees know what to expect. I would say I project assertiveness and a positive attitude when communicating with my staff, but I'm also flexible.

Good managers are skilled in the art of communication and sensitive to the different personality styles of their employees. With some, you adapt a more outgoing style; with others, you must be reserved and careful or they will feel threatened. There are cues and constant feedback from the subordinate. A good manager knows how to read these and respond properly.

You develop communication skills by listening, not just by hearing. It becomes second nature to adapt your own style to that of the person with whom you are speaking. This is the fastest way to get on the same wavelength and avoid misunderstanding. It takes a little more effort on the manager's part; but I've seen the results, and they are definitely worth it. Management theorists call this "pacing." You need to align with someone before you can lead him or her.

When acting as the communications link between your staff and superiors, representing your department to upper management and upper management to your department, the best communication style is one that is open and honest and that allows others the freedom to question.

Much of the success in the corporate environment depends on clear communication of company goals and directions—and on listening to feedback. Fostering good communication is one of my top priorities.

9. What steps would you take to terminate an employee who is not performing adequately?

First, I'd make sure I followed all applicable company rules and procedures and any laws that govern the given situation.

People should have at least one warning and a chance to improve their performance. I would counsel confidentially and give a written warning covering a specific period of time, along with clear guidelines for improvement. Then I would watch carefully and be sure to acknowledge and praise the employee for a sincere effort to remedy the situation.

However, if counseling and warning fail to produce results, I would not hesitate to terminate the employee. Firing is probably the hardest thing a manager does because you come to know your employees as people. But, when someone who is notified that his or her work is below acceptable standards won't take steps to save his or her own job, the manager must protect the company. Again, I would make sure that my actions were properly documented and that justifiable cause for termination was shown.

10. What plan of action do you take when facing a problem?

Before I act, I think. I try to distance myself from the problem so I can look at it objectively and analyze all sides. Sometimes I even write it down to see it more clearly.

When I've reached a decision, I present my planned solution to the people affected by it or to those who must carry it out. I get their input, incorporate any suggestions that are appropriate, and then we implement the plan.

I believe in immediate but realistic solutions to problems. Ignoring them rarely makes them go away.

11. After you've made a decision, do you stick to it?

Generally, yes, because I have found that my problem-solving and decision-making methods work. But I am flexible, and when a proposed solution clearly isn't getting the expected results, I modify. Sometimes a minor change will make a major difference.

12. What experience have you had supervising people with advanced degrees?

(If you have had experience:)

I've supervised highly credentialed professionals in (one/several) of my jobs, specifically _____.
The work I was required to supervise and evaluate was very specialized. In many cases, I learned from them as the work progressed. It is very stimulating to work with highly educated people.

(If you have had no such experience, but you don't want to rule out your potential ability in that area:)

To date, my work has not required me to supervise people with advanced degrees. I do have experience working with people who hold graduate degrees in _____ (engineering/law/accounting/science/psychology) and have acquired through association with them much knowledge about their work. I would be very comfortable supervising postdoctorate professionals. I am confident we could develop a relationship of mutual respect. I would always respect their greater knowledge of specific areas of the work; but I think they would come to respect me for my even-handed and broad-based management skill.

13. **(Did/Does) your staff come to you with personal problems?**

My staff knows my door is always open, but they also know my number-one priority is getting the job done right and on time. They have come to me with personal problems in the past only when those personal problems might interfere with work progress. I have shown sympathy, but my advice and solutions have always been offered with the company's goals in mind.

14. **(Did/Do) you run your department only "by the book?"**

In many companies, management style is dependent on corporate culture and company philosophy. When that philosophy dictated a very strict interpretation of rules and procedures, I adhered to it. But there are many situations not covered by the book, and in those situations my judgment was guided by the particular situation and the department's mission. My main goal is to get the work done by people who perform their jobs with energy and initiative. It's very difficult to write how to do that into a policy manual.

15. **Have you ever been in a position to delegate responsibility?**

Delegating responsibility is one of a manager's first priorities. No matter how great or small my assignment,

I developed a system for the work to go on even when I was not there. I prepare competent people to take my place successfully when I move on. This is one of the most difficult jobs a manager has, because it can interfere with his or her feeling of being indispensable. But only after you train someone to assume your duties are you ready to move up.

16. **Have you ever been responsible for the profit-and-loss statements?**

(If yes:)

Yes, my position as _____ at _____ involved direct responsibility for the bottom line. I had the authority to make decisions that would affect the company Ps & Ls in the areas of _____, _____, and _____. During the time I held that position, the company realized _____ _____ (a XX percent increase in gross/net profit, or a similar statement; choose and rehearse language that sounds objective and uses percentages).

(If no, but if you do not want to rule out your potential skill in this area:)

I have never been directly responsible for the bottom line in the sense that management would come to me and ask me to explain why profits were not as projected or expected. However, my work has required me to keep an eye on methods that would produce efficiency and improve the overall financial picture of the company, and I have accomplished that with success. I would welcome both the responsibility for bottom-line results and the authority to make decisions that would improve the P & L.

17. How well do you manage people?

I've experienced good results from the people-management side of my work. I can communicate company goals and motivate people to produce. More than that, I've seen and tapped potential in my subordinates that even *they* didn't realize existed. I'm pleased that (many/several) of those I initially trained and supervise eventually moved on to positions of greater responsibility in other departments and areas. This is a private legacy, and I'm proud of it.

18. What makes a good department head?

Good communication skills are an important part of department management because the department manager acts as a communications conduit both from management down and from the people in the department up.

A good department head must be able to internalize corporate goals. Then he or she should apply them to the work in his or her department, using those goals as a guideline for making decisions, assigning priorities, and developing new projects.

Effective management of any department—large or small—requires the same management skills used in directing a larger segment of the organization—an entire division or facility. These skills are difficult to acquire, but they're highly transferable from one situation to another.

Chapter

6

Career Objectives

DELIVERY

Your career objective should vary, depending on the target job. For this reason, you shouldn't indicate one on your resume, and you should be careful about what you write down on an application form. Don't write the *real* one down either ("getting this job"), even though that's what it is.

The key to determining your objective is to find out as much as you can about the job and the employer *before* the interview. Do your phonework: Making a few anonymous phone calls to the personnel or hiring department is the best way. The usual telephobia subsides once you start.

Don't speak to the person who will be interviewing. Just find out general information, such as the job title, the supervisor's title, how the position relates to other jobs in the company, and so forth.

If you're responding to an ad, use it, too. But be careful about taking it too literally. The employer is *paying* for responses. The ad might hire only *quality*, but it advertises for *quantity*. The result is a wish list—a construct of an ideal candidate, who could be developed only by a genetic engineer.

Call first. Listen carefully, and develop an objective that is ambitious, but realistic. Then you can throw the objective dart right at the bull's-eye. Most other candidates won't even hit the target.

If the interviewer is nursing a wound when you walk in, one of those aimless candidates probably just skipped past you in the hall.

SCRIPT

1. How important to you is the opportunity to reach the top?

It's more of a general goal than a constant ambition of mine. I know that, if I'm the best employee I can be, career advancement will take care of itself. Having a goal without hard work is like aiming at a target without ammunition. Working hard and enthusiastically is the best method for reaching the top.

I complete my work to the best of my ability and trust that, if I prove myself to be an asset to my employer, I'll be rewarded. So although the opportunity to reach the top is important to me, I know that opportunity presents itself only to those who earn it.

2. Why do you want this job?

Because of the challenge and the opportunities at _____. I'm well qualified for it, and this is exactly the kind of _____ (competitive/creative/progressive/technically oriented—use an adjective appropriate to the company and type of work) atmosphere I've been looking for. My career goal is _____, and this job would allow me to develop my potential further while actively participating in that kind of work.

I've been offered a number of other opportunities; but, after evaluating those jobs and companies, I decided not to make a move. Making a job change is a major decision, a long-term commitment that I take very seriously.

After researching the history and future plans of _____, meeting people who work here, and seeing the kinds of jobs there are to be done, it seems like a perfect fit!

3. How long will you stay with the company?

As long as I continue to learn and develop my capabilities. As with any partnership, I intend to fulfill my commitment and meet challenges as they come.

It's my hope that, as long as I perform well on the job and make contributions, I'll be considered a valuable employee. And as long as I'm making a contribution that is valued, I'll have no reason to leave. However, if for any reason I don't meet the company's expectations, I don't expect to remain on the payroll. So I look forward to staying as long as I'm productive.

4. What do you picture yourself doing (five/ten) years from now?

Five years from now, I see myself working for this company. My job will have increased at least one, probably two levels in responsibility and scope. I'll have made a significant contribution to the _____ _____ department and will be working on new

ways to _____
_____.

Ten years from now, I will have progressed up the ladder into general management. I'll have gotten there by proving I'm a producer, a problem solver, and someone who can grasp the scope of a program while not losing sight of the details.

5. What are your long-term career objectives?

(Give specific details about the field or profession first and then about the level you hope to attain within it.)

Essentially, I have given my career and opportunities a great deal of thought, and from that process I've developed a plan for achieving my long-term objective. This position is an important step in that long-term plan.

6. Are your present career objectives different from your original goals?

Slightly. I made my plans at an early age. However, I modified them as I progressed and learned more about my capabilities and the work.

For a career plan to be useful—like any business plan—it must be flexible enough to respond to changes in the world of work. Career planning is an ongoing process, and several times throughout the years I have revised and updated my goals in response to new developments and opportunities.

7. Would you consider a switch in careers at this point in you life?

Possibly. I'm very happy with my chosen field, have done well in it, and think there are things I can do even better as I progress upward.

However, I believe in being flexible and open to new opportunities. If you have a position in mind for me in the company that is different from the work I've been doing, I'd like to explore it. I'm always interested in seeing how my background and skills can contribute to my success at a particular job.

8. Would you be willing to relocate in the future?

(If the answer is an unqualified "Yes":)

Definitely, yes. When I have moved or relocated in the past, new worlds of opportunity opened for me. Any major change, while always containing some risk, is a chance to grow, learn, and advance. All I need is a few days' notice, and I'll be ready.

(If the answer is a *qualified* "Yes":)

Yes, if that relocation provided opportunity for advancement or for making a greater contribution to the company. My family is very supportive of my career. They know I would base such a decision on whether the move would be advantageous for them, too. I would evaluate the opportunity carefully; and, if it were good, I'd need a little time to complete my commitments—both on the job and at home—before getting settled somewhere else.

(If you would rather not:)

My family and I have established our roots here. It's a great place to live, and we've made many friends in our community. Stability and continuity are important for raising a family.

I'd never reject a transfer without considering it seriously, however. I'd base my decision on whether the result would be a net gain—for the company, for my family, and for myself.

9. Do you want to be president of this company?

Yes. I don't know too many capable, ambitious people who don't aspire to the highest management level within their companies. I aspire but I perspire, too. It gets better results.

I also realize that there are many other steps along the way through which I can learn, contribute, and be rewarded in my work. I want to do the best job I can, moving on to the next challenge when I'm ready. If I continue to do that, I'll automatically rise to the top.

10. Did you want to be president of your (current/previous) company?

Yes. Whenever I think about my goals and plan how I will achieve them, I aim high. However, I'm also a realist and know there can be only one president.

Being president of my (current/previous) company would have given me the opportunity to carry out plans and ideas for improving and enhancing the company, its operations, and its products. But wherever I've worked, whatever the scope of my position, I've done that to some extent.

11. Would you like to have your (current/previous) boss's job?

Yes. I think a major part of any good employee's job is to contribute to the department's work and efforts in a way that reflects on the department manager's skills and abilities. When that happens, the manager often is targeted for promotion.

Helping my boss get promoted might result in my being considered for his or her job. In that sense, I guess you could say I'm interested in my boss's job.

For companies to grow and improve, the people who work there must grow and improve. Promotion and advancement within the ranks are signs that a company provides opportunities and recognizes the potential of its employees.

12. What kind of business would you like to own?

I wouldn't like to own a business right now. I'm committed to my career, and that means working in another organization and helping it meet *its* goals.

I have considered what business might be interesting to own after I've accomplished all I can in this industry and retired. It would probably be something related to my outside interests, such as _____

_____.

13. When do you expect a promotion?

I would like my career to continue progressing as well as it has in the past. But I'm a realist. I know promotions aren't given, they're *earned*. When I've mastered my present position, improved it with my ideas, prepared myself to take on new responsibilities, and trained someone to take over my job, I'll be ready for a promotion.

14. How much thought have you given to your future?

I think about my future on a regular basis, but in a practical way, rather than just wishing. I consider my attributes—my abilities, skills, and experience. Then I determine how I can combine them into an action plan.

Occasionally, I update my plans in response to new information and opportunities. But I don't let them interfere with giving all I've got in the present. You don't improve the future by wasting time in the present. You get to it by making every day count.

Chapter

7

Suitability for Target Job

DELIVERY

Suitability for a job is really just specialized use of certain learned information and practiced skills. Almost everything we do on the job (even a highly technical one) is *common sense*. Ask any supervisor and you'll find out how few employees specialize in that!

If you've done your phonework (preinterview phone sleuthing), it's just a matter of matching your background and skills to the requirements and duties of the target job and selling the interviewer on your suitability for it. Then, combine your unique background, experience, and qualifications with the interviewing skills you're learning here, and the job offers will follow. Just don't flub your lines.

SCRIPT

1. **If we offer you a position and you accept it, how soon thereafter can you begin to work?**

   After giving my current employer two weeks' notice. As long as I know what's expected of me, there's no reason I can't plunge right into the new job. Procrastinating has a way of draining energy, which I could channel into my new job.

   I have the enthusiasm and energy to get started. I'd also enjoy meeting the people I'll be working with so we can develop a positive working relationship right away.

   Some people like to take a vacation between jobs,

but a vacation should be earned. I might have earned a vacation on my last job, but I intend to prove myself here at the earliest opportunity.

2. Would you be in a position to work overtime if required?

Absolutely. A job is a lot more than a paycheck—it's a responsibility. I can understand that some people like to leave their work at the office and finish it the next day. But when I'm given a task to complete, I do so as soon as possible, even if it requires that I work overtime.

When I've been given the responsibility for a job, I take it seriously. I make sure what needs to get done gets done. Whether I'm compensated for overtime or not, I derive personal satisfaction from the extra effort that results in success.

Extra effort makes the difference between a good job and a better one.

Questions 3 through 9 are job-search research questions, requiring research into the industry, the company, and the specific position or positions available—that phonework I mentioned earlier. If you're aiming at a public company, call ahead and request a copy of its most recent annual report. If it is a private company, request a brochure, catalog, or product spec sheets that will help you learn more about the company's profile, programs, and products.

There are other resources that can be used, such as *Standard & Poor's Register of Corporations, Directors, and*

Executives; Moody's Industrial Manual; Thomas Register of American Manufacturers; and others. Head for your local library and the reference librarian for assistance.

3. What do you know about our company?

(Do your job-search research, and single out two or three positive facts about the company, like growth in recent years, increasing market share, and innovative breakthroughs. Print these facts neatly on cue cards—3-by-5 inch index cards—for rehearsing your script. Just don't take your cue cards into the interview. You might also want to include any other information you picked up during your research, such as:)

Most important, I've heard that _____
_____ (name of company) offers a challenging work environment that expects a great deal from people and gives them the opportunity to realize their potential. That's what I look for in an employer—an active, creative environment where I am limited only by my capabilities and where positive results are acknowledged.

4. What do you know about the position we have open?

(Again, demonstrate your initiative by offering a few facts about the position you couldn't have learned from the advertisement.)

5. **Who do you think are our three major competitors?**

I'd say _____ because
_____
_____;
_____
because _____;
and probably _____ because
_____.

6. **Do they have any advantages over our company?**

(Although you want to show you are aware of competitors and their products, be careful to balance any complimentary remarks about them with equally complimentary remarks about the employer. For example:)

I understand that _____ has a higher market share in the _____ line, but _____'s recent introduction of _____ is already being received favorably and should surpass the competitive products within the next 12 months.

OR

_____ is well established, large, and has a higher sales volume, but _____ has the advantage of being more aggressive, innovative, and—it appears—more efficiently managed. You've already made impressive inroads into their customer base. In the marketplace, _____ has the giants worried.

7. **What three trends do you see in the future for our industry?**

(Take the time to prepare yourself for such a question, and be sure you can name three trends. Try to choose favorable ones. The following example would be suited to an employer in the communications industry.)

First, as our economy has developed away from manufacturing and toward service jobs, the urgent need for better communication between people has become obvious. While the volume of paper increased steadily, communication—meaningful interaction—decreased.

Second, communications companies provide an indispensable service to people everywhere, helping them understand each other better. In the business environment, increased communication results in a better understanding among associates, employees, and customers. There's a definite trend toward more use of the services of companies such as _____ by all kinds of businesses to help them identify their needs and enhance their ability to meet them. There's a great potential for growth.

Third, the trend to desktop publishing should streamline operations in companies like this, decreasing cost and improving turnaround time to the customer. Whereas some believe customers will invest in their own equipment and render our industry obsolete, there's little evidence this is happening. In fact, there's a trend toward increased use of outside service companies like _____ to avoid the high cost of full-time employees.

All in all, the future looks very bright for this industry. That's why I'm here.

8. What interests you about our company?

I've been very impressed in all the reading and research I've done about _____. It projects an excellent image, and its message is persuasive. Internally, it's a sound operation, with ambitious goals and realistic plans for achieving them.

I see great potential for growth here, and I want to be part of it. I have many ideas that I know could be implemented here better than anywhere else.

9. What single thing about our product or service interests you most?

(As before, you must be prepared for this one. Know something about the company and what it does, such as:)

I understand your computer systems have the least maintenance downtime of any on the market. For an account executive, that's an important sales advantage.

You're offering the customers more value and efficiency for their investment.

OR

You just introduced an innovative life insurance package, and you're the only company in the industry that offers benefit flexibility like that. I'd like to be able to work with a creative organization whose products offer its customers the leading edge in life insurance protection.

10. Do any of your friends or relatives work for this company?

(Some companies have policies against nepotism—hiring friends and relatives of employees—even for unrelated positions. If your answer is "Yes," and you know you're interviewing at a company with such a policy, honesty is still your best response. Your answer is a matter of company record, and you could be dismissed if you misrepresent even in an area as seemingly insignificant as this.)

11. Why are you interested in this job?

Because it offers everything I've been looking for, both in the position and in the overall environment. It fits perfectly with my career plans.

Everything I've accomplished in my career to date has prepared me to perform the job you need done. My background in _____, my experience with _____, and my training in _____ uniquely qualify me to perform this job better than anyone else.

You won't find a better candidate or a more dedicated employee.

12. Why would you be happy doing this type of work?

Because it's the kind of work I've always enjoyed doing. All the tests I took early in my career said I was best suited for this kind of work. I agreed and made my career plans accordingly.

Someone who likes his or her work demonstrates enthusiasm, initiative, and energy that others can't match. There's a great law of life that few people realize: We like most what we do best, and we do best what we like most!

13. In what specific ways will our company benefit from hiring you?

It will be getting someone whose skills and training most closely match the job requirements. Further, it will be getting the benefit of my experience at _____

_____, _____, and

_____.

My background relates directly to the position be-ing considered and is a primary reason why it will take me less time to produce than someone who hasn't had as much direct experience.

I'm dedicated and learn quickly. I try always to ex-cel at what I do. So, when you hire me, there's little risk you'll be interviewing for the job again soon.

14. How did you learn about this opening?

(Your answer should demonstrate an active, thoughtful job search, not just a weekend scanning of the want ads.)

I responded to your ad in the _____ edi-tion of the _____, but for some time prior to that I had been investigating this company as a poten-tial employer. I was intrigued by your _____ _____ and your _____, and I determined that I really had something to offer here.

I made a few initial contacts and learned more about the company; then, when your ad appeared in the newspaper, I thought to myself, "What timing! This is a perfect match." And here I am.

15. What do you believe are your special qualifications for this job?

(Begin by mentioning any specific training and experience that apply to the position. Then:)

As a result of my background, I have direct insight into the requirements of this job and know how to increase _____ (efficiency/productivity/sales).

Further, I'm driven to achieve, to surpass my most recent record, so you'll never see me turn in a merely acceptable performance. I really think, from all you've told me, that the position could use someone with my attributes. There are a great many challenges to be met, and the right person—someone who approaches them with energy and determination—will achieve results greater than anyone thought possible. I believe I'm the right person.

16. Do you feel confident in your ability to handle this position?

Absolutely. I'm familiar with the basic job requirements, and I learn quickly. It should take me only a short time to become familiar with this company's procedures and methods.

If I don't have the answer to something, I find it. The sooner I learn what is expected of me, the sooner I can excel in the job. I don't like to waste time when there's a job to do.

It undoubtedly will require extra time and effort on my part in the beginning; but I'm more than willing to devote that time and effort because it enables me to do the job right the first time.

17. Will your military experience benefit your job performance?

(If your military experience is directly applicable to the duties of the position:)

Yes, my training and experience in (electronics/materials handling/communications) is directly related to performing this job.

Throughout my military duty, I was continually required to accomplish sixteen hours' work in an eight-hour day. Most of the time we put in twelve hours and more.

You can take the (two/four/six) years of military experience on my resume and effectively double it. That's how intensive it was. Some people have one year's experience two times. I have (two/four/six) years' experience twice!

(If your military experience is not directly applicable:)

While my *duties* as a _____ (munitions officer/decoding expert/mess cook) might not appear related to the duties of this position, everything else about my military experience helped prepare me for the job.

In the military I learned responsibility, discipline, and hard work. Because military pay starts out low, I drove myself to exceed the requirements for promotion and advancement. As a result, I rose rapidly through the ranks. Those skills have served me well throughout my career, and I know they'll serve this company well if I'm hired.

18. How do you manage to interview while still employed?

I'm using personal time that I've earned as a result of rarely taking sick leave. I manage my interview schedule, and I try not to be away from my job more than one day at a time.

Sometimes it means working extra hours, but I take my responsibilities seriously. No one has to cover for me. In addition, I check in through the day for messages and to see if any situations need attention.

I've developed a system for the work flow. As a result, no order sits on my desk, and nothing is delayed in my absence. Employees do themselves and their employers a disservice by getting themselves overloaded or in a position where they are the only ones who can do a job. If you take care of the little things, the big ones take care of themselves. A little organization, self-discipline, and prioritizing go a long way.

19. How does the fact that you are a recent college graduate benefit our company?

I have a wealth of knowledge I've acquired over the past four years, and I'm anxious to get started using all I've learned. I'm already trained in new methods and procedures, so I should be able to implement them immediately.

My college education was a very full-time job. With classes, studies, exams, papers, and special projects—all in addition to my part-time job to help support myself—I worked constantly. I had to make every hour count, so I became adept at time management and planning.

No one supervises you in college. You know whether you've been successful when your grades are issued. There are long periods between evaluations, so you must be self-disciplined and budget your time.

I have the latest training and skills and the willingness to get the job done.

20. Do you feel you are ready for a more responsible position? Tell me why you think so.

Yes, definitely. When you cease to be challenged, you stop growing. I've gone as far as I can go in my present job. My manager is very pleased with my work, but the _____ (size of the company/present economic environment) limits additional responsibility in the foreseeable future.

I know I am capable of greater achievements, which is why I'm interviewing for this position. There's a challenge offered here that I'm ready to meet.

21. Is there one particular trait or skill you possess that should lead us to consider you above other candidates?

(Think about your answer to this question in terms of your particular abilities and how they apply to the target job. Then tell and sell.

Are you a fast typist or programmer? If the job involves customer service or is otherwise people oriented, do you have the ability to make others respond favorably? In the lines provided, formulate the first part of your answer, being sure to mention what you think is the most prominent of your own unique and proven skills. Then close with the scripted paragraph that follows.)

_____

_____

_____

_____

_____

_____

_____

_____

In addition to that, I have the drive to take on this job and to do it well. In fact, I think I'll excel at it.

22. Do you have your own tools?

(If yes:)

Yes, I do. The right tools, used skillfully, improve the quality of the work. I've invested time and money selecting and maintaining quality tools. They go where I go.

(If no:)

I don't have a complete set of professional-quality tools for this kind of work, because they were provided in my past jobs. I would be willing to make the investment, however, because the right tools used skillfully improve the quality of the work.

23. Do you have any questions?

(Be ready for this one. Listen carefully throughout the interview, and ask incisive but benign questions when given this opportunity [see Chapter 12, Questions to Ask the Interviewer]. This is not the time to inquire about things like salary and benefits. You're right for the part, but don't bring up the contract before the director offers it to you. Questions relating to the structure of the company, duties of the position, or nature of the product line would all be appropriate here. For example:)

Yes. You mentioned you'd be expanding your Albuquerque packaging plant, which would result in about 100 new positions. Is that due to a move away from outside packaging suppliers and to in-house handling? Is this a test, or are there plans for more of this kind of expansion?

OR

Yes, I have a question regarding the organization of the department. You mentioned this position reports to the director of customer service, but you also remarked that it falls within the authority of the marketing department. Is there also a director of marketing to whom I would report? If so, where does the company divide the duties and responsibilities of each director? Is there any overlap?

(A final note: Make sure you're comfortable with your topic before asking the question. Don't ask a question just to have a question handy here. If it was a lengthy interview and all of your questions have been covered, it is perfectly all right to say:)

I had many questions, but you answered them all. You've been so helpful, I'm even more excited about this opportunity than when I applied!

24. May we contact your present employer?

(If your employer does not know you are interviewing, smile—don't giggle—and say:)

No. I haven't told my employer. So please let me know before you contact anyone there. Once there's a firm offer on the table, or you've narrowed the field to only a few candidates, the information I've given you can be verified.

My boss deserves the courtesy of hearing I'm leaving from me. (He'll/She'll) be upset, but I'll assure (him/her) that everything will be done to accomplish the most efficient transfer of my duties. You'll probably get more than a reference—you might get a testimonial!

(If your employer knows you are interviewing and would give you a good reference:)

Yes, my employer knows I am interviewing and understands the reason. We've had a good working relationship for the past _____ years. But now I've reached the highest level possible there, and I've trained people to assume my duties.

My boss regrets not being able to offer me more at this time and understands that I'm not working to my full potential. We're parting on good terms. (He/She) even told me recently, "That's the price you sometimes pay for hiring and training the best people." All of what I've told you will be confirmed when you call. But please let me know first so I can let (him/her) down gently.

25. Do you know anything about (bookkeeping/printing processes/and so on)?

(If yes, give a brief summary of your experience and skill level, plus:)

I'm looking forward to learning more in this area, particularly the _____ system you use here. I've heard it is the most efficient, state-of-the-art method. I'm a quick study and know I would pick it up fast.

(If no:)

I don't have specific experience in that area, but I have a great deal of related experience that will help me learn quickly. I have a natural ability for _____ (numbers/computers/manual dexterity/sales), which I'm confident will enable me to learn the job in record time.

26. Are you willing to start as a trainee?

(If you are willing to accept an entry-level position:)

Yes, definitely. This is a new area for me, and I believe in getting a good foundation in the basics before progressing. I also have a great deal of knowledge and work experience, which I'm sure will contribute to my rapid progress through the basics. If I learn at my usual rate, I expect to be assuming greater responsibility when it becomes available.

(If you already know the job, and taking a step backwards would not be in your best personal or professional interests, try to leverage that knowledge like this:)

I've had ____ years of background in this field already. While I know I'll need to learn the specific methods and procedures this company uses, I'm a trained and experienced person.

I'd be wasting your management's time as a trainee, and that wouldn't be in the company's best interests.

The knowledge I bring with me qualifies me for the higher level position of _____.

27. Are you looking for permanent or temporary work?

(You wouldn't like to be looking for a permanent position and find yourself hired for a job that lasted only six months. So understand the employer's point of view. Don't take it too seriously, though. After all, *life* is a temporary assignment!)

I'm looking for permanent work, a position with challenge and responsibility, that will allow me to develop as I meet those challenges and handle that responsibility.

Temporary work is for people who haven't decided what they want to do with their lives. I have a carefully considered career plan and am looking for the right company that will help me fulfill that plan—while *I* help *it* grow and become more profitable.

28. In five minutes or less, tell me why this company should hire you.

(What an opportunity! Portions of what you will answer might have been covered in your answers to earlier questions, but here's a chance at center stage for five whole minutes! That's about as long as the average sales presentation. You're getting a chance to screen-test using a role you play every day! So develop a succinct, convincing sales presentation, and don't forget to close with a happy ending.

Use the following sample presentation for a job as a sales representative with a pharmaceutical company to get ideas for your five-minute monologue. Pay attention to the words and phrases in italics: They are examples of effective use of interview vocabulary. Then write your own presentation in the lines that follow this sample answer and rehearse it!)

You need a *self-starter* who can handle a large territory and deal regularly with a variety of people—from hospital purchasing agents and directors of nursing to private physicians. You need someone who can take objectives and *systematically meet* them using *creative* approaches.

I've *proven* my *ability* to work with people and numbers and to handle big responsibility with a minimum of supervision. In my previous sales work, I usually *exceeded* my quotas. Further, I filed my paperwork on time, *expediting* order processing and shipping. I'm a high-energy person who doesn't leave until the work I have to do is done.

My employers have always been satisfied with my sales totals. Just as important, my customers were always pleased with the follow-up, support, and service I offered. These things are crucial to succeed in this business. When you're dealing with medicine and other pharmaceuticals, your customers need to know there is someone available to answer questions and to deal with problems that might arise in patient application. I'll work hard to establish a presence with the doctors and hospitals.

The customer contact and public relations experience I gained from my other, nonsales, jobs will also help me deal with all the different personalities I'll encounter on a daily basis.

Finally, my degree in biology gives me the scientific *knowledge* to understand the technical aspects of this product line and to discuss it intelligently with physicians and other health-care professionals.

(The close:)

Based on this, my *ability, experience, skill,* and personality *match* the *requirements* and diverse *responsibilities* of the position. Most of all, I really *want* this job. I know time will confirm your decision to hire me.

(Now, you write the script. You'll be surprised how easy it is. After all, you're writing about your favorite subject—you! Welcome to center stage. Spotlights on! Get ready for a standing ovation when you're through.)

_____

_____

_____

_____

_____

_____

_____

_____

_____

_____

_____.

29. What makes this job different from your previous one?

(Only *you* can answer this question with specific differences in job requirements and duties. That's why it's imperative that you know the target job well. If there are differences, list them; then:)

Jobs are like people: If two people focus on their similarities rather than their differences, they get along better and accomplish more. If I focus on what I know and can do, I'll learn the less familiar tasks as I go along, and I'll be contributing right from the start.

30. Why do you want to enter this field?

From the research I've done, there appears to be tremendous opportunity in this field. The possibilities seem limited only by the imagination and energy of those in it.

I want to spend my career in an industry and a company where the horizon is always expanding, and there is always new territory to cover. When I wake up in the morning, I'd like to anticipate the possibility that I'll learn something new or solve a problem I've never faced before—one that will require all my talent.

In summary, I want to be where things are developing, changing, and growing. And I want to make a meaningful contribution to that development and growth.

31. What do you think about how we run our operation?

From everything I've seen and heard, I'm very impressed.

From my outside research, the way my first telephone inquiry was handled, and our discussion here, I see a vibrant, responsive organization. A good measure of a company is in the enthusiasm of its employees, and the people here sure demonstrate that.

32. Do you think your lack of _____ (a degree/experience) will affect your ability to perform the job?

(No degree:)

No, I don't think it will have an adverse effect. Even though I might not have the traditional academic letters after my name, I've learned a great deal, both in my job and on my own, that will help me perform the duties required by this job.

Education is an ongoing process throughout life. I have a great deal of respect for formal education, and I acquired all that time, money, and circumstances would allow. But I find myself learning all the time. When it comes to my job, I'm very practical: If something will make me better at what I do, I want to learn all I can about it. If it won't, then it can wait.

I'm confident I have the knowledge and skill to get

the job done and even to find new ways of doing it more efficiently and effectively.

(Lack of experience:)

Even though I might not have years of experience in this profession, I have the knowledge necessary to make an impressive start and the willingness to learn and improve. I have the skills required by this position. I learn quickly and will work hard to prove myself.

Sometimes employers can do better when they hire people who don't have a great deal of repetitive experience. That way, they can train these employees in their methods and ways of doing the job. Training is much easier than untraining.

And when you're required to prove yourself, there's a healthy tension at work, like the mainspring that moves a watch. When that spring releases, momentum is working in your favor. I think you'll be impressed by how quickly I learn and how much I accomplish in this position.

33. Aren't you overqualified for this job?

Although I already know the job we're discussing, my background will enable me to eventually expand it into something more. I might be *more* qualified than others you're considering, but every job can be enhanced by being creative.

With my qualifications, I can do the job right away. Then the company will benefit from my additional experience, and I'll be able to do more with the position than has been done in the past. In that way, I'll continue to be challenged—and you'll be acquiring someone with additional potential.

I've learned many techniques for improving the efficiency and productivity of this type of operation. I'd welcome the opportunity to use what I know to improve things here.

So while I might be starting out at a slightly lower level of responsibility, this company is growing and going places. I see a lot of opportunity here.

Chapter

8

Salary Negotiations

DELIVERY

The rule of thumb is: Don't discuss salary until you've been given a clear indication that you're the preferred candidate (or one of a short list). Yet this rule can be tough to follow, and diversionary tactics can quickly develop into something of a power struggle between you and the interviewer—which is not what you want. Salary negotiations should be the starting point for your *employment* with a company, that is, ideally, you will have been offered a position before talk of money begins. Of course, the operative phrase here is "should be," because unfortunately, often salary negotiations may begin before you even walk across the company's threshold—most commonly, on an application form or during a screening interview over the phone with a representative of the human resources department of the company, who has been instructed to do some preliminary weeding of the candidates. Your goal is to not show your hand until you have a clear idea of what the position is and what the employer thinks it—and you—are worth; the employer's goal is to save time, and potentially money, by establishing as quickly as possible an opening bargaining position.

Note It's important to distinguish between salary history and salary requirements, because they really are two separate issues. Salary history should be (but isn't) illegal to ask about (after all, what does another employer's idea of your value have to do with this employer's assessment?). Even if it had some marginal significance, benefits and job duties are never the same.

It goes without saying that you'll be expecting to earn more in the target job than in your current position, so when you're asked for your salary history, make sure you know what you're actually earning. Yes, that's what I said: *Make sure you know what you're actually earning.* You'd be surprised how many people don't. Though everyone can tell you what his or her monthly take-home pay is, many don't realize that, when calculating annual income, he or she should factor in nonsalary compensations, which include medical benefits, stock options, overtime, bonuses, profit-sharing and retirement plans, and others. These factors can add 25 percent or more to your salary.

The question regarding your salary requirement may seem like a trap just waiting to be sprung. The chances of your answering too high or too low when asked this question (whether on an application or in person) are almost one to one. As I said above, your goal is to keep your options open as long as you can, to enable you to drive up your value and knowledgeably state an amount satisfactory to you and the employer. I don't know of a single case over the past 20 years when an employer rejected someone before an interview for not stating a specific salary requirement on a resume or application. Yet I know of hundreds of applicants whose salary numbers excluded them. Applicants concerned with being able to pay the rent/mortgage don't realize how negotiable salary is to employers. Even the most structured compensation systems allow for hiring above the stated rate range.

Artificial salary constraints are a great negotiating tool, but they rarely stop employers from getting someone they want. Don't let them stop you. Instead, after reading the following salary questions, which will test and hone your negotiation skills, adapt the answers to fit your situation and your style.

SCRIPT

This chapter's Q&A is divided into two sections, to address two very different scenarios: The first addresses the very difficult situation of being asked salary questions in the early moments of the interview, before you've had a chance to describe your suitability to fill the open position or even to find out the responsibilities you would be expected to assume in the job. The second scenario addresses the preferable situation: You've been told you're the candidate of choice, or that you're one of the top contenders for the job.

Scenario 1

If the interviewer puts you on the spot at the beginning of the interview by asking you one or both of the first two questions, your best bet is to try a diversionary response to gain time to learn more about the position and to open the way for a discussion about your experience and capabilities.

1. What salary are you hoping to make in this position?

At this early stage, without knowing the details of the position, it's almost impossible for me to cite a fig-

ure. Perhaps you could tell me at least the broad para-
meters of the position and the salary range that has
been established at this company for this position. In
my experience, similar or identical job titles at various companies don't necessarily mean the same thing,
and I'd really like to know how the job is described here
before attempting to put a dollar figure on it. Furthermore, future opportunities at a company carry as much
weight with me as salary and current job description,
and both those factors will impact my salary requirement.

(If the interviewer continues to pursue the salary
topic before you've had a chance to sell yourself, you
may have to cite a figure to avoid annoying the interviewer and thus being eliminated from consideration
simply because you were unwilling to respond to this
line of questioning. If you're put in this spot, your preinterview preparation will enable you to make as informed a response as possible, and one that is in your
best interest.)

2. What is the salary you think is appropriate for someone with your experience?

I've determined that my responsibilities are com-
mensurate with the high end of the salary range most
employers are willing to pay for this position, which is
$_____ to $_____.

3. What is your current salary? Or what is your salary history?

I understand your need to know this information, and of course, I'm happy to tell you, but I'd be more comfortable if you'll allow me first to explain what my current responsibilities are, then ask what the responsibilities of this position are, to better enable both of us to determine if the two positions can really be compared monetarily.

For me, job fit is as important as money fit, so I'd like to avoid boxing myself in or being excluded at this early stage because of salary restrictions—either mine or yours.

(If you feel you cannot avoid giving an actual figure:)

OPTION 1

My current employer pays me $____, which is at the high end of the salary range at the company, and attests to the level of success I have achieved.

OPTION 2

Though my current salary is $____, which is lower than many other companies are paying for similar work, it is not a reflection of my work, but rather a reflection of the fact that my current employer is a small (or startup) firm just beginning to gain a foothold in this area, and therefore salaries are necessarily lower. I do, however, also receive a yearly bonus and stock options.

OPTION 3

My current base salary is $____, but with overtime, end-of-year bonus, company-matched savings plans, pension, and profit sharing, I earn $____, which doesn't account for the complete medical coverage benefit at my current company.

Scenario 2

In this scenario, we assume you've made it through the interview process and that either you've been presented with an offer or it has been made clear the employer is about to begin the salary negotiation process. Though this is the ideal position to be in (the employer has a good idea of your value and you know what will be expected of you if you accept the offer), these, too, can be treacherous waters to navigate, in particular if the first scenario has been played out—that is, you were forced to cite salary figures early in the interview process.

This scenario can be further broken down into two sub-scenarios—we'll call them 2a and 2b. The first puts you squarely in the hot seat; the second at least gives you a launch point. Both situations, however, may be impacted by two factors: (1) what you have or have not already revealed about your current salary or salary history and expectations, and (2) whether the offer is made in person, over the phone, or via mail or e-mail.

Scenario 2a

If your potential employer has made it clear that you're the candidate of his or her dreams, but is still unwilling to show his or her hand regarding money, the opening line in this sub-scenario may go something like the following.

1. **Your professional experience and personal demeanor seem to be an ideal match for both this position and this company; what we need to find out is whether we can match the salary you are looking for. What are your salary requirements for accepting this position?**

   (As in scenario 1, you can try putting the ball back in the employer's court first, again, to give you more information to work with. If the opening question comes over the phone or via mail or e-mail, your first move is to request a personal meeting to discuss this important issue, where you'll have the benefit of body language cues. Reminder: You should have done your homework, to determine what the standard salary range for the position is across the industry. Thanks to the Web, getting this kind of information has never been simpler.)

   I'd prefer to hear your opening offer, based on your knowledge of my capabilities and experience, in conjunction with your knowledge of the salary cap for this position at this company.

   (If you did not have to reveal this information during scenario 1:)

2. **What is your current salary, and what percentage increase do you expect to make?**

Note Never lie about how much you're currently making. Don't forget: Employers have access to the same tools—in addition to personal contacts—that enable them to check any information you provide.

(Here, too, your preparatory research will stand you in good stead. Be honest about what you're currently making, including nonsalary factors, and then base your desired increase on what you know to be the going rate for the job title and whether the new position is a promotion from your current post.)

My current yearly salary, including bonuses and benefits, is \$_____, and I am willing to accept a 15 percent increase over that.

(If the move is a lateral one, most employers expect to offer an increase of 10 to 15 percent, so asking 15 percent at the outset will allow for the all-important wiggle room. If, however, the position is a promotion and/or involves relocation, increase that percentage based on the new title and the new location. For example, a move to San Francisco's Silicon Valley from Des Moines, Iowa, is going to mean a huge rise in your living expenses.)

Scenario 2b

This is the best position to be in: You've been able to avoid giving any—or too much—information regarding your salary history and/or requirements; the employer has made it clear you're the person they want for the job; and an offer is on the table.

1. We're prepared to offer you $_____. How does that meet with your needs/expectations?

(If the offer falls short, either of what you're currently making or the percentage increase you were expecting to make:)

Though I'm very excited about the job and the professional opportunities it holds, I am disappointed in your offer. I'm currently making $_____, which includes _____, _____, _____, and _____, and to make the move, I'd need to increase that by at least ____ percent.

(At this juncture, many counteroffer scenarios are possible, and it is beyond the scope of this or any other book to cover them all, but here are some guidelines. If the employer counters with, say, a base figure that meets your current salary, and adds stock options, you'll need to base your decision on what those options might be worth. Is this a startup that is short on cash but that shows real promise of huge growth in a reasonably short period of time? Is this an established, successful, and still-growing firm whose stock you'd be foolish to turn down?

You'll also need to base your decision on your personal situation. Are you cash poor now because you've just bought a house—or will have to do so because accepting the job will require relocation to a higher-cost area—and therefore need your salary in the form of a biweekly check? Again, preparation is all-important. You should have learned, for example, how the company's stock has been doing. And at this point, it's fully appropriate for you to ask the questions regarding company benefits because, as discussed, nonsalary benefits can add as much as 25 percent to your real salary, and so will impact your decision to accept or to continue negotiating. See Chapter 12, "Questions to Ask the Interviewer.")

WHEN ENOUGH IS ENOUGH

One of the most important strategies of the salary negotiation process is to know when to *stop* negotiating. You don't want to talk yourself out of the job. It's important to keep your goal in mind—which presumably is to get the job—not win some game of dollars and cents.

Use your common sense to determine when to stop, based on your preparatory research and your interactions so far with the employer. If you have compromised as much as you are willing or can afford to, and the employer is clearly unwilling or unable to offer more, it's time to say "thank you," accept the offer, and move on. Remember, you will be working with these people, and they won't forget how you handled yourself during this important process. And of course you may choose to reject the offer, if you feel—reasonably—that you can do better elsewhere. This is not a one-way negotiation; you are interviewing the company as much as they are interviewing you.

Chapter

9

Experience and Training

DELIVERY

Experience isn't what you've done; it's what you *do* with what you've done. Everyone who is the same age has the same amount of experience—it's just that each person has it in different areas. Those different areas are really just matters of *focus*.

Even nontraditional experience can apply to the requirements of the target job. As you prepare for your interviews, take an experience inventory. Be sure to include knowledge and skills gained from part-time jobs, volunteer work, and community service.

Training is everywhere: adult education programs, community colleges, university extension courses, trade or technical schools, and correspondence courses. If you want to acquire new skills—or brush up on old ones—to meet the requirements of the job you've targeted, get the training you need without delay. Just be sure the course is skills oriented (no theory unless you need it for the job), inexpensive, and short enough to give you a certificate of completion within a few months. Anything longer is unlikely to make much difference in getting hired.

But if you have set career goals that will require longer training—such as completion of a bachelor's or graduate degree—go for it. The long journey begins with that first step. In the meantime, explore job opportunities at lower levels in the same field. If your ambition is to be a registered nurse, apply for an entry-level job in a hospital or clinic. By the time you've completed your course of study, you'll also have several years of related experience and will be all the more valuable in your target job.

Employers *say* they want people with potential. But reality doesn't yield to rhetoric. They want *skills*. Usually *yesterday*.

SCRIPT

1. How did you get into the type of work you are doing now?

(The first part of your answer should include specific information about the career path that led you to your present job. Rough out your script in the lines provided. Then close with the scripted paragraph that follows.)

_____

_____

_____

_____

_____

_____.

Considering my educational background, my interest in _____, and the satisfaction I derive from completing a job properly, I decided to become a _____.

I don't think I'd be able to really excel if I weren't truly interested in the job or if I were merely motivated by its financial rewards. However, because I find the work both challenging and fulfilling, the better I do, the more I enjoy it.

2. What have been the biggest frustrations in your career?

I've always approached my career with enthusiasm, so I really haven't experienced much frustration. The primary annoyance on the job is from fellow workers who don't seem to be interested in performance, only in their paychecks.

It isn't that everyone should live up to my standards, but hard work and respect for others are common denominators for any successful team. Beyond that, the primary motivation should be to excel—to find ways of doing things better, faster, and more effectively.

However, when I find myself up against a source of annoyance, I convert it to an opportunity to prove myself and set an example for others to follow. It has worked very well—for them and for me—because enthusiasm is contagious.

3. What have been the biggest failures in your career?

While I honestly can't recall any major failures, I've had a few temporary setbacks—mainly when I tried to do too much at once. There are times when we're called upon to produce more results in less time. When you work at maximum production anyway, it's unrealistic to expect a week's work to be done in a day without the quality suffering.

In one instance, when I was given an assignment

that was long on work and short on time, I tried to complete twice the work by the deadline. It was impossible. Fortunately, I accomplished enough to make the project successful. But I learned that no one, including me, can consistently produce optimum results with that much self-imposed pressure.

I've benefited greatly from the experience and have become even more effective in my work than before. Managing time and establishing priorities can make any employee more effective.

4. What risks did you take in your previous job and what was the outcome?

In my previous job, it appeared that the only way to succeed was to drive myself and those around me to the limit of our potential. If you're afraid to try something new, you've unnecessarily foreclosed other options. But if you're willing to attempt another way, more might be accomplished. Our hard-driving approach turned our department into a responsive, respected part of the company.

At times, being creative can be risky. My risks have always been carefully considered. I took them only after making sure I could save my employer money or time by my action. Because I put careful thought into my decisions, the outcome was consistently positive, and my success was noticed. By the time I left, I had the reputation of being an innovator who knew how to get the job done.

5. **How (do/did) you like working for your (current/previous) supervisor?**

Working for my (current/previous) boss (has been/was) a great experience. (He/She) (is/was) a dedicated professional who really (understands/understood) this business and how to be successful in it. As a result, (he/she) (has earned/earned) the loyalty and respect of the entire department, and I (will be leaving/left) with mixed emotions.

From the time I began working at _____

_____ (name of company), my supervisor took a sincere interest in my work. Under (his/her) guidance, I grew personally and professionally. I've learned that a great working environment is a two-way responsibility. All employees have to work together and respect each other for the job to get done.

I've been fortunate to work with and learn from someone who trusted and believed in (his/her) subordinates. That trust gave me the confidence I needed to be successful. I plan to use that same leadership style when I supervise others.

6. **Have you done the best work you are capable of doing?**

That's hard to say, because I'm always striving to do better; but my performance reviews were consistently excellent. I've often tested my limits and found I was capable of more than I—or my employers—thought.

There are times when, for various reasons, it becomes difficult to do your best work. At times like those, I found myself driving to produce, to maintain my record of success. I approach every assignment with all my energy and talent. Even if I've done it before, I regard it as a new challenge to be met with a fresh approach.

I guess I've succeeded, because the results of my work have always been well received.

7. Why are you leaving your current position?

I need to be challenged to develop my potential further. I'm interested in additional responsibility and new opportunity, which unfortunately are limited at _____ (name of current employer) because of _____ (company size/limited product line/company restructuring or downsizing).

The reputation and market focus of _____ _____ (name of prospective employer) offer many opportunities for someone with my training and experience. It's the optimum kind of environment I've been seeking.

8. What three areas of your job do you like most?

Only three? That's difficult to answer because I like everything about my chosen field. Rather than pick out little details of the routine work, here are three general things.

First, I believe in the _____ (product or service) and its value to our customers, so that's a major one: a sense of pride that we're doing something important.

Second, I like the constant challenge to all my faculties—intellectual, emotional, and physical—that working in this field provides. It keeps me active and productive.

And third, it's the sense of progress—knowing that we're in a growing, dynamic industry that will be important for many years. I'm excited about my participation in the future.

9. What three areas of your job do you like least?

I really like this work, so I can't think of any major dislikes. I guess my answers will have to come under the category of "nuisances" or "annoyances." They're inevitable when you're trying to accomplish something.

The biggest annoyance is other people who don't share the same sense of purpose or care about the company's goals—the kind of employees who are just putting in their time. It happens everywhere you work; but I can't help thinking that, if everyone would concentrate on the business at hand, we'd all accomplish even more.

Then there's the usual paperwork that seems to slow down the action. I realize the importance of documentation, and I cooperatively fill out the forms and log in all my time and phone calls. But I'm always looking for efficiencies in that area that will get me out (on the floor/in front of the customer/in the field) where I belong, doing my job. I'd rather be on top of my paperwork than the other way around.

Finally, under the category of "nuisances" is

_____.

(Mention something trivial but common, like back-orders from overseas suppliers, computer systems that need updating as soon as they are installed, and the like. Smile good-naturedly to show you realize "no pain, no gain.")

10. Describe the best supervisor you ever had.

My best supervisor was someone who expected a lot from me and taught me to expect a lot from myself. Then, (he/she) guided me through the training, knowledge, and experience I needed to fulfill my potential and become a credit to the company.

(He/She) didn't overmanage, but let me make enough minor mistakes on my own so I'd learn by doing. We discussed assignments—what was required, what I needed to do it, and where I could find assistance—but then (he/she) let me do my work my way.

There was always a feeling of mutual respect and trust. (He/She) fought for (his/her) employees, but (he/she) never tolerated anything less than the best job possible. As a result, (his/her) people always knew (his/her) expectations and internalized them so little direct supervision was required.

With such a firm, fair, and consistent leader, a lot of typical coworker dissatisfactions and disagreements were avoided. I remember that as a time when we showed that teamwork could accomplish a great deal. It was a pleasure to go to work in the morning and leave at night with a sense of accomplishment.

(If you're applying for a management position, the final paragraph in this answer is also applicable:)

I'm fortunate that I met this extraordinary person early in my career. Knowing (him/her) really helped me develop my own leadership skills. Whenever I encountered problems in managing others, I thought about what (he/she) would do in the same situation. If I couldn't come up with an answer, I'd call (him/her) and ask. Although it's been ____ years since we worked together, (his/her) methods serve as a strong guide for my own leadership decisions.

11. **Describe the best company you ever worked for.**

(Think carefully about what "best company" means to you as an employee and develop your script from your experience. Write it in the lines provided after the following two samples.)

The one where people worked long and hard, but enjoyed themselves doing it. There was always a sense of purpose, and of achievement, in the air. At the end of every day, I had a real feeling of accomplishment and looked forward to the challenges awaiting me the next morning.

OR

The one where there were no arbitrary lines between management and staff, but rather a team of skilled professionals all working together. People respected each other, understood what was required of them, and did their jobs to the best of their unique abilities. It was always "you and me against the problem," rather than "you against me."

The really exceptional companies I worked for recognized people as a resource and made a conscious effort to acknowledge and reward people for their work. In that way, employees felt they were needed and were motivated to do their best.

(Now, your answer:)

That would be _____
(name of company) because _____

_____
_____
_____
_____
_____
_____.

12. Describe the best job you ever had.

(As with your response to Question 11, think about this response in relation to your own experience. Do you want a steady work flow and no surprises? Do you thrive on challenge, change—even chaos?

Because you're aiming at the target job, know what that job requires and describe one very similar. If your description of your best job is the complete opposite of the target, you'll be shooting off your toes. Most companies have stretchers for emergencies like that. Your get-well card will be "No-interest Letter No. 2." Here's a guideline to hit the bull's-eye:)

My best job was the position of _____ _____ at _____ (name of company). It offered me the opportunity to use all my initiative and skill to solve problems and get things done. At times the pace was fast, but things were never out of control. Beneath it all were organization, structure, and guidelines that helped employees make decisions and accomplish their jobs effectively.

Defined policies and procedures, combined with encouragement to use creativity in my work, are what characterize a great job for me.

13. What references would your (current/previous) employer give you?

I'm confident that all my references will be favorable and will confirm what we've discussed here today.

(If you suspect that any unavoidable reference might be negative, and you've *really tried* to correct it, here's a sample answer. Rehearse it carefully, because this is a preemptive strike to minimize the importance, objectivity, or validity of the bad rap.)

The majority of my references will be favorable,

but you might not find that to be the case with
_____ (name of supervisor/
company). Although I'm proud of the work I did there,
and always did my best, my supervisor and I never
seemed to overcome some philosophical differences.

I tried to be accommodating, and I learned a great
deal about interpersonal relationships from my attempts. Finally, I decided (his/her) philosophy was getting in the way of our productivity, and I chose to leave.

I gained a lot of useful knowledge and experience
on that job, which I use every day in my work now. It
was just one of those things that happens occasionally
even in the most successful careers. I made the best of it,
cut my losses and moved on. Even though people know
they should consider the source, few really do. Therefore, I wanted to let you know in advance.

(Now, your answer:)

_____
_____
_____
_____
_____
_____.

**14. How would you compare the quality of your
work to that of others in the same job?**

The quality of my work has been consistently as
good as—or better than—that of my coworkers. I've always met or exceeded expectations.

Some people pay too much attention to the work that others around them are doing. If they're doing more, they lower their speed to the average. I'm just not that kind of person. I set my pace according to what is required by the job, and I always try to beat the clock and my own record.

People spend more time on the job than anywhere else. I owe it to myself and my employer to make every minute count. If I just kept doing the average work, at an average pace, life would be awfully boring. So I don't wait for challenges to be dropped in my lap. I go out and find them!

15. How would you compare the quantity of your work to that of others in the same job?

Like the quality of what I've produced, the quantity of my work has generally exceeded expectations. My output was as high as—or higher than—that of any coworker.

There have been times, however, when it was necessary to temporarily set aside quotas to improve quality. As organized as I am, there have been times when I've needed to (fix manufacturing problems/devise a new work-flow program). Temporarily, the output was reduced so we could improve overall operations.

It was always time well spent that paid off in the long run. We don't expect our machines to run indefinitely at peak efficiency without maintenance, and we can't expect that of systems either. If we didn't take time out to take care of the exceptions, eventually we'd get nothing done.

16. In what areas of your current job are you strongest?

(Think about your strengths, and script your answer in the lines provided. Use the sample answer as a guideline, but make your answer specific to the work you do and the target job.)

My strengths come from my energy and my ability to find the fastest, most efficient way to get the work done. As a result, I'm able to keep increasing my output while maintaining the quality.

One of my other strengths that supports this is how well I get along with others—supervisors, coworkers, and subordinates. Because I communicate well with people, I get the support and cooperation I need in my work. I try to be sensitive to the many personalities with whom I work. Each has different needs and is motivated by different things.

(Now, your answer:)

_____

_____

_____

_____

_____

_____

_____

_____

_____

_____

_____.

17. **In what areas of your current job are you weakest?**

(Remember, you're here to sell yourself *into* a job, not out of one. Avoid revealing any major weaknesses. If you have them, you plan on eliminating them anyway, don't you? Leave them in the lobby. Just mention something benign that shows you're human *before* you take the pre-employment physical.)

I don't have any major weaknesses that interfere with how I do my work. The only area where I occasionally fall behind is in completing my daily activity reports.

Sometimes, I find myself with two or three days' worth of reports to do at once. If that's the case, I stay late and get them done. I have a good memory, but I also keep careful notes in my calendar as I go along; so I always have the information I need to fill them out accurately if I do fall behind.

(Now, your answer:)

_____

_____

_____

_____.

18. **What factors contribute the most to your success on your current job?**

First, experience. The training and situations in my previous jobs helped me go further and faster on this job.

My jobs have increased in responsibility, with each level building on the last.

Second, continuing education. In addition to formal schooling, I've always taken the time to be informed and current on what I needed to know to be effective. I attend seminars and workshops and take courses, and I always have professional or management materials available to read when I'm waiting somewhere.

This leads me to the third reason for my success: good planning and productive use of time. When I run into roadblocks on the job, I figure out a way to eliminate them or at least turn them into speed bumps.

Wasting time while you're waiting for something to happen drains energy. If Plan A is temporarily on hold, I immediately swing into plans B, C, D, and so on. It's amazing how much nonproductive time can be turned into job improvement if you're just aware of how to do it.

19. What do your supervisors think are your strengths?

From what they've told me informally—and formally during performance reviews—they think I'm a productive and efficient employee and a good team player.

I've had particularly high ratings in meeting objectives, completing assignments on time, and working well with coworkers to accomplish company objectives.

20. **What do your supervisors think are your weaknesses?**

(Prepare an answer here that mentions some trivial matter. In most performance reviews, supervisors find it necessary to pinpoint some area that needs improvement. Like teachers, supervisors hesitate to give anyone a perfect score.

Again, don't mention any mortal sins, only minor correctable and *corrected* items. Tardiness, absenteeism, negligence, and poor attitude are all mortal sins to be avoided. Instead, confess to something like:)

Although my evaluations have been overwhelmingly favorable, I have occasionally received comments about needing improvement in the area of _____ _____ (record keeping/filing/ expense accounting).

It's not that I don't meet the requirements in those areas. It's just that sometimes I get so intent on achieving something major by a certain deadline that, occasionally, these routine functions are delayed while I'm immersed in a major project or problem.

Eventually I catch up, however. Supervisors don't like to give employees a perfect score, so occasionally something like that appears on a performance review.

21. **What is your current boss's title, and what are his or her duties?**

(Sample answer:)

My supervisor's title is supervisor of sales support. (He/She) reports to the national sales manager and is responsible for overseeing the work of the department, which consists of five sales coordinators and a clerical staff of three.

The department is responsible for supporting a national sales force of 25, preparing the salespeople's correspondence, processing orders, making sure salespeople follow up on all leads, and maintaining distributor relationships.

As the senior sales coordinator, I also have responsibility for special projects, such as tracking samples given to customers and reporting on the results of their use. In that function, I report to the national sales manager, who is responsible for the sales force's meeting its objectives.

(Now, your answer:)

(His/Her title is _____. (He/She) reports to the _____ of _____, and has responsibility for _____

_____

_____

_____.

22. Describe a typical day in your job.

(Sample answer:)

I arrive early to review my list of objectives for the day, which I prepared before I left the previous night. I assign priorities to my work, so the most important and necessary tasks are accomplished first.

There are many interruptions throughout the day. The phone rings, and suddenly there's a fire to fight. It's unavoidable. As long as I've established a good plan, I keep those objectives in mind, and accomplish them one at a time between all the emergencies.

I stay levelheaded. Everyone takes their cues from me, so I'm positive, organized, and congenial. No matter how difficult the task seems, the work gets done, the problems get solved, and we make progress.

No day is really typical in my job; there's always something new. But good planning and time management skills help me stay on top of the work, so my coworkers and I enjoy meeting new challenges while we keep the department moving along.

(Now, your answer:)

_____

_____

_____

_____

_____

_____.

23. What do you consider the single most important idea you implemented in your current job?

(Spend some time in a careful review of your previous jobs. It is human nature to forget achievements and to focus on what we haven't achieved. One way of always having your achievements handy is to write them down as they happen. Whenever you solve a problem or create a more efficient method for doing something, write a sentence about what you did on a business card; keep these in you wallet where you can refer to them often.

As you add to the deck, insert the older ones in a business card holder. In addition to sensitizing you to your own value, it's a great source to help you update your resume. Employers want to know more than who you *are*—they want to know what you've *done*. That's how they decide what you can do for them. Here's an example of the presentation:)

Shortly after I became a clerical supervisor at _____ (name of firm), which employs 20 attorneys and 10 secretaries, I determined that the lawyers were still writing most basic pleadings in longhand, with legal secretaries merely transcribing them. Yet, most of these documents had common elements. There was a lot of duplication of effort, and some brilliant analysis by the attorneys was only being used once before it was filed away forever.

I compiled a file of pleadings that I thought could be stored in a retrieval system, and I produced a cost analysis for the firm's partners to review. They accepted my proposal after analyzing it thoroughly. Then I researched the best word processing system for our use, negotiated the terms of a lease, and supervised the installation. The project took about six months from start to finish, and I invested a great deal of overtime but the results justified the effort.

Now all attorneys have a five-inch binder of pleadings organized by categories. When they need a motion or other court document, it's just a matter of making a photocopy, filling in the blanks, and sending it to the clerical department. Other documents are being added continually.

I also created a work-request system to monitor and assign priorities to the work, rather than using overstuffed in-baskets where the work was handled on a last-in, first-out basis. Now the clerical department can turn around anything from a one-page motion to a hundred-page brief in half the time, error free. As a result, the firm has been able to increase its legal staff to 25 attorneys, with no accompanying increase in clerical staff. Billable hours have increased by 40 percent.

(Now, your answer:)

_____
_____
_____
_____
_____
_____
_____
_____
_____ .

24. **How would you install a _____ system?**

(In the first interview with the personnel type, specific qualifications usually are not probed thoroughly.

However, there might be one or two questions like this one, and you should be prepared. If you know the answer, relate it in a logical, organized step-by-step way. Don't be an expert who can't communicate what he or she knows. On the other hand, if you don't know, don't ad lib. Try this:)

I haven't had experience with that specific system, but I have installed a similar one, the _____ _____. I'd check the manufacturer's literature to determine the differences between that system and the one I know. Then I'd proceed to _____

_____
_____
_____
_____.

25. What specific strengths did you bring to your (previous/current) job that made you particularly effective?

(Sample answer:)

When I became marketing director of the textbook division, I had the advantage of knowing the books, because, in my former job as development editor for the company, I supervised their production.

So I concentrated on matching products to markets. As my research revealed other products we could launch to increase market share, it was easy to work with the product development people because I'd been there. I understood their creative and schedule needs, and they appreciated working with a marketing person who didn't make unreasonable or uninformed demands.

My extensive experience in all areas of production and distribution was my greatest asset. It enabled me to be practical and to capitalize on additional opportunities to increase sales dramatically.

(Now, your answer:)

_____

_____

_____

_____

_____

_____

_____

_____

_____

_____.

26. What specific strengths do you think you can bring to this position?

(Sample answer:)

My education in _____, my experience in _____, and my knowledge of the area of _____ all will contribute to my performing this position with little or no downtime. I have the proven ability to transfer my skills from one job to another.

Because of this, I can learn my way around an organization quickly. I can concentrate on motivating and managing the staff, while developing relationships with other supervisors.

27. Would you recommend your (previous/current) place of employment to others?

Certainly, depending on the kind of work they were seeking and their attributes. _____ _____ (name of company) is a sound, viable operation. There is interesting work there for people who can produce.

As I might have mentioned before, I am seeking another position because my growth there is limited by _____ (company size/downsizing). But someone at a lower level might have many years of productivity and challenge ahead.

28. Can you explain the long gaps in your employment history?

(This is a tough one. If there are long gaps, your answer should offer a brief, believable explanation, and then you should convince the interviewer why this won't affect your ability to succeed at the target job.)

When I was younger, the decisions I made seemed

right at the time. Although these choices don't appear on my resume, I learned a lot along the way.

In one case, I believed I needed more education and training to achieve my goals, so I left work and re-enrolled in college. That decision was justified because, when I returned to the work force, it was at a higher level of responsibility and pay. Not only did I learn critical skills, but I learned the self-discipline that formal study requires.

Another time, I had the opportunity to serve on board a three-masted schooner on an expedition in the South Seas. While being a deckhand didn't add to my computer programming knowledge, I learned the value of hard work, team effort, and overcoming hardship. Everyone should learn those values. It really helps to supercharge a career.

I've had life experiences I can bring to bear on the job. My track record for the past _____ years has been consistent and progressive, and my work has increased in responsibility.

I have set my career goals and developed a plan for achieving them. That, combined with my family responsibilities, makes me a very stable employee and a good risk.

(Now, your answer:)

_____

_____

_____

_____

_____

_____

_____

_____

_____

_____

_____

_____.

29. What was your first job and how did you get it?

(Sample answer:)

My first job was as a carrier for the daily newspaper in my hometown. I was 12 years old, and my mom wasn't sure she wanted me out in the predawn hours. The circulation manager wasn't sure I was old enough either. I asked them to give me a chance. Then I invested in reflectors for my bike and a loud horn that I could use if necessary. It could be heard from anywhere on my route. That satisfied my parents, and they gave me permission to take the job.

I handled that route for three years, rarely missing a day. I eventually built it up to the number-one route in the paper's circulation area. I won several sales contests, even a trip. The circulation manager many times told me how glad the was he took a chance on me. My parents were very happy with how my college savings account grew over those three years.

That job taught me more about responsibility and self-discipline than the part-time jobs I held through high school. I was in charge. I considered myself a route manager. I even kept a notebook with all my customers' preferences. You know, "Mrs. Jones wants her paper in the milk box," "Mr. Adams wants his inside the screen door." I still have that notebook—somewhere. That job gave me the first great sense of satisfaction in doing a good job. It's something I value to this day.

(Now, your answer:)

_____

_____

_____

_____

_____

_____

_____

_____

_____

_____.

30. How would you sell me that chair next to you?

Before I'd sell you on buying it, I'd learn all about the features and benefits. Then I would learn about you, your company, the chairs you are now using, and your needs. I'd determine what advantages my product had over your current chairs—price, quality, comfort, durability, or design—that would appeal to you.

Then I would determine if you were the decision maker to whom I should make my presentation. If so, I'd make an appointment to meet with you and discuss your office furniture needs. In that discussion, I would listen carefully. Then I'd make you aware of needs you hadn't realized before.

For example, I would say, "Mr. Jones, my research reveals that your office staff lost 210 days last year to lower-back injury and pain. I'm not saying your current chairs caused that problem, but they aren't designed to alleviate it either. Our chair is designed with lumbar support to cushion and ease the pressure on the lower back that often results in injury and chronic back pain.

It is a more cost-effective product than your current chair because it is designed to last 10 years—twice as long as the chairs you are now using. And, it can potentially save you thousands of dollars per year in downtime and employee medical benefits."

Notice I didn't make any unsupportable claims. I said, "potentially save thousands." I made you, the customer, aware of needs you might not have considered when purchasing office furniture. Then I positioned my product to meet those needs. When I was convinced I had secured your agreement to what I was saying, I would ask for the order:

"Mr. Jones, how many of your current chairs would you like to replace at this time? My volume discounts make the price of our chair even more attractive when ordered in quantities of more than five dozen. When you consider how well employees respond to their employer's providing them with new, quality fixtures and equipment, I think you'll agree it would be a wise move to replace them all at the same time.

From my count, I see you currently have 65 chairs in use. I would be happy to remove the old chairs for you when we deliver the new ones. Would the first of next month be a convenient date to take delivery?"

31. Have you ever walked out on a job?

(If no:)

No, my responsibilities to my work and my family are too important to simply walk out in frustration. In the past, when I saw a negative situation that was beyond my control, I carefully planned my exit, secured another position first, and gave my employer adequate notice to allow a smooth transition to my replacement.

(If you have quit one job before securing another:)

There was a time when I made a rather painful decision to leave one company before I had secured a new position. This resulted from working very hard, putting in long hours, and trying to turn a negative situation around without any cooperation.

As long as I was in that job, I couldn't get away to interview for a new one. If I left, even for a day, the work wasn't done. I'd lost my sense of perspective. Finally I gave my notice, leaving only when I found and trained my replacement.

Then I took some time to evaluate my options, assess my abilities, and get my career back on track with the *right* position. I secured the ideal job within six weeks. By that time, I was rejuvenated and tackled my new assignment enthusiastically.

When I look back on the job I left, I see that nothing since has even approached its difficulty. After what I learned there, I know I can meet any challenge.

32. Have you made any contributions to publications in your field?

(If yes:)

Yes, I have. I've had articles published in the _____ issue of _____ and the _____ issue of _____.
I have copies of them right here in my briefcase that I'd be pleased to give you, if you'd like.

(If no:)

Not yet. But I have some ideas for articles and several outlines. My knowledge of the field and my writing skills have progressed to the point that I'm comfortable completing the articles and submitting them for publication.

33. What do you consider the most significant accomplishment in your entire career?

(Remember, "significant accomplishment" doesn't necessarily mean a breakthrough discovery or a major financial success. Even a personal accomplishment that improved your professional stature or an idea that made the work of others more pleasant or efficient is worth mentioning. Think about all you've done in your career. Read the sample answer. Then script yours in the lines provided.)

My most significant accomplishment was rising from the steno pool at _____ (name of company) to become its administrative assistant. I worked there two years, and my only education beyond high school was a nine-month certificate course at a business college. But I knew I was capable of more than shorthand, typing, and filing.

I continued to work hard by day while taking night courses in business administration at the community college. On the job, I asked about more responsibility and opportunity. Then, one day I had the chance to prove myself by volunteering to coordinate our company's annual employee fund drive. I invested hundreds of extra hours over a six-month period. My effort and initiative were rewarded when the funds collected turned out to be the highest in the company's history.

As a direct result of the recognition I received from my volunteer success, I asked to fill the administrative assistant opening. A few years later, I broke into the management ranks. I've since completed my degree and accomplished many things in my career. But I still look back on that one event as the turning point and the accomplishment that made all the others possible.

(Now, your answer:)

_____

_____

_____

_____

_____

_____

_____

_____

_____

_____.

34. How did you get into this type of work?

(Your script must be personalized. In preparing it, include information that shows your decision-making ability and your willingness to accept challenges. Don't say, "I got lucky." After all, the best definition of _luck_ is "when preparation meets opportunity." The harder you work, the luckier you get! Study the sample answer for ideas:)

I was employed as an assembler at _____ _____ (name of company) for two years, when a position opened in the materials handling division for an administrator. My coworkers teased me when I applied for the position. They thought it wouldn't be possible to assume a desk job.

Even my (husband/wife) was skeptical. (He/She) knew I wanted to make more of myself someday, but I'd only begun night courses in business and didn't have the formal qualifications for the job as it was posted. What I did have was a strong belief in myself, and a track record of accomplishment and dependability.

To everyone's amazement, I got an interview, and another, and another. Management was also surprised that someone from the shop floor knew as much as I did about the company's product and the system for turning raw materials into finished goods. I sold myself hard for that job, and I got it. I remember my exact words: "Who's better in the war room than someone who's been on the front lines?"

I'll tell you, it was tough going for a while. I felt slightly insecure about not having my degree yet and in awe of everyone else in the front office who seemed so sure of themselves. But I soon learned that the ability to make intelligent decisions wasn't something that came from a book. Besides, I knew more than they did about how our product was manufactured and about the problems manufacturing faced when we used materials that didn't meet the specifications.

One promotion led to another. Eventually, I obtained a degree and entered the ranks of general management. I never lost my practical perspective from manufacturing, and I never lost touch with the people who really make the company—those who produce the product.

By moving from labor to management, I opened the door for others to follow. Today, that company has a much more integrated and people-sensitive approach than its competitors, which is one reason for its success. I don't mind taking a small measure of credit for that.

(Now, your answer:)

_____

_____

_____

_____

_____

_____.

35. What has been your biggest disappointment on the job?

There haven't been many things I can point to as disappointments. In one case, I worked for a company with a product that could really make a difference in helping the lives of many. I saw great potential there, believed it could be realized, and worked hard to make it happen.

But it just wasn't meant to be. Improper management decisions, inadequate capitalization, and downright creative bookkeeping, as they say, led the company into debt. It's a shame because the world lost a potentially great product.

In terms of my own career, I turned that disappointment into a valuable lesson. I'm sensitive to the danger signs that signal that a good organization is heading for trouble. As I gained more and more responsibility through my career, I've been able to call upon my experience to keep history from repeating itself in other places.

36. Why did you work in civil service for so long?

I didn't think I needed to make a change. I knew I was doing something worthwhile, was progressing in job responsibility, and liked my work.

Some people think an executive must change jobs every three or four years to remain fresh. But in many jobs, experience and longevity make you more effective.

I prefer to innovate on the job wherever I am. I don't look for a new job according to an arbitrary timetable. Instead, I keep improving in skills and knowledge. When I reach a dead end in the career path, as I finally did in that job due to funding cutbacks, I move on.

37. Have any of your employers ever refused to give you a reference? If so, please explain.

(A refusal to give a reference can be more damaging than a poor reference. Your explanation for such a situation should be brief, believable, and matter-of-fact.)

Yes, once. I worked for _____ (name of company) for _____ years when I received a better offer from a competitor. The opportunity for growth at the new company was so much greater, and the working conditions so much better, that I didn't see any other choice but to accept. In fairness to my then-current employer, I gave (him/her) a chance to match the offer, and (he/she) refused.

But my decision to leave made the first employer angry. The owner of the company believed in loyalty to (him/her) at all costs and despised the competition. It really didn't matter to my new employer that my present employer wouldn't give me a reference. They knew my abilities and qualifications, or they would not have recruited me in the first place.

I don't even know if (he/she) still refuses to give me a reference. To my knowledge, the situation hasn't had any effect on my employability since that time.

38. Have you had a chance to upgrade your skills to the level currently required?

Yes, now my skills and abilities are well matched to the requirements of this job. I don't think a day has passed in my career that I didn't improve my skills to some extent.

I'm comfortable with my ability to handle this position with only a very brief orientation into the company's specific procedures. From there, I hope to continue improving and expanding my skills and abilities here at _____ (name of prospective employer).

39. Have you ever sustained a serious injury on the job?

(This is an attempt to ascertain if you've collected worker's compensation benefits in the past and if, as a result, you're a risk to the company. If you did sustain an injury from which you are completely recovered, explain briefly and honestly without indicating you're accident prone.)

In _____ (year), I was injured when _____ _____ (a chain broke and a girder fell on me/noxious fumes escaped

while I was inspecting a construction site/and so on).
My medical records show that those injuries have completely healed, and my physician approved my return to
my former job. I haven't had an incident since.

40. Does your current employer know you are interviewing?

(If no:)

No, I decided not to discuss the matter until my
search resulted in an offer of employment. My work
record has made me a valuable employee who'll be
missed, and I didn't want to create any morale problems.

I don't intend to entertain a counteroffer from my
present employer. I've considered my decision to look
for another job very carefully. There's simply nothing
my present employer can offer me at this time, so I'll
wait until it's time to give my notice and help them find
a qualified replacement.

(If yes:)

Yes, my employer recognizes that they have no position available that would allow me to continue growing.
They're happy with the work I'm doing. But I've trained
my staff well, and there are several ideal candidates for my
position. They deserve a chance to move up, and I need to
use more of my potential than I'm currently using.

We're parting on good terms. I'll always value the
experience I acquired there and will be able to use what I
learned throughout my career.

41. Why have you had many jobs for short periods of time?

(Your answer should explain the reason, then emphasize your future plans for more stability in your work record. Convince the interviewer your job-hopping days are over.)

(Sample answer:)

Early in my career, I made several changes after short periods of time. In one case, I accepted and entry-level job on the basis that I would be promoted within six months. After a year of working below my capacity and receiving no response several times when I asked to be moved into the position promised, I realized I'd need to move out to move up.

In another situation, my department was reorganized shortly after I was hired, and I was moved into an unrelated position that didn't fit my background and skills. I tried to make it work for six months, but it was obvious there was a mismatch. I did a good job, but I just wasn't happy. It wasn't my field.

Since the beginning, I've charted a definite course for my career. I looked for positions that fit my skills and abilities, where I could really contribute something. In those earlier jobs I mentioned, I found myself in positions that I didn't fit in, through no fault of my own.

In every job, I've given my best effort and made it work. In recent years, my work record has been more stable. That's due in part to the lessons I learned. I'm more careful now to be sure I'm going after something that will work out for my employer and myself.

Employers and employees should work together to make the best match possible. Their commitment should be long term so they both derive maximum benefit from the relationship. Anything else is counter-productive.

(Now, your answer:)

_____

_____

_____

_____

_____

_____

_____

_____

_____

_____ .

42. What is the highest accomplishment you can name from each of your previous jobs?

(This answer should contain information specific to your job history. In the space provided, write the most significant accomplishment you can think of from each of your previous jobs. Use the sample answer as a guide:)

In my first position as a management trainee for _____ (first employer), I devised a system for handling customer orders that reduced the average waiting time from six minutes to four minutes per customer. We were able to increase sales during rush periods by 30 percent. As a result, my system was adopted for use companywide.

As a district manager for the same company, I instituted employee incentive programs for customer service. In a survey by our regional chamber of commerce, consumers in our area named us the friendliest fast-food chain.

From there, I took the position of director of marketing for _____ (next employer). At the time, it was a start-up company with no name recognition facing formidable competition in the athletic shoe market. I recommended we target the children's market, which was just beginning to boom.

My strategy used television advertising during children's viewing hours. We offered premiums—kites, balls, and other sports equipment—with the purchase of shoes. Within one year, we were the fastest growing youth shoe manufacturer.

Looking back, all my major accomplishments resulted from doing something better. I developed fresh, creative approaches to old situations. I've had unique insight into the operations of companies I've worked for. I regard them as flashes of intuition centered around common sense. Others call them ingenious—I call them innovative.

(Now, your answer:)

_____
_____
_____

_____
_____
_____
_____
_____
_____
_____
_____.

43. Did you change any of the job duties in your current job after you began it?

Yes. Initially, my strategy is to follow the job description until I'm sure of my responsibilities. Then I start to evaluate.

I look at all the work I'm doing and decide which tasks can be handled more efficiently by delegating them to lower salaried support personnel. Then I can concentrate on increasing the bottom line.

In a recent management consolidation, I found myself temporarily covering the assignments of three other managers. When I assessed their various duties, I found I could handle all the management decisions that involved getting new programs up and running— while a team of four clerks administered existing programs.

We eventually hired one new manager. (He/She) and I have divided the work once done by four high-salaried individuals. The company has saved over $100,000 this year alone as a result of my restructuring improvements.

44. In what areas have you received compliments from your superiors?

I have always had high marks in job effectiveness, initiative, and enthusiasm. Because I look at each assignment as a potentially exciting challenge, my managers say I create excitement in my department. That spirit is contagious. It results in a greater team effort, less absenteeism, and higher output.

45. Did your company increase its (sales/profits) this year?

(Even if your job is not related to sales, knowing the answer will demonstrate an awareness of the bottom line. Be optimistic. You always want to appear that you're working for a winner. Two typical answers are given.)

Yes, sales were up 10 percent in the last quarter, and 18 percent over the last three quarters from the previous year. Net profit as a percentage of sales increased from 8 to 10 percent. We've had a very good year.

OR

As the customer service manager, I don't have ultimate responsibility for sales. But my work is important to customer satisfaction and repeat business, so I'm included in all sales meetings. Our actual sales figures are not published, but we're enjoying a record-breaking year.

46. Have you ever been fired?

(Be grateful if your answer to this is a simple "No." If you have been fired, your explanation should be upbeat, carefully prepared, and thoroughly rehearsed to accentuate the positive, even if you can't eliminate the negative. For example:)

Yes, I was terminated from the position of _____ (title) at _____ (name of company) in _____ (year). Although I didn't take issue with it at the time, I was let go based on incorrect information.

I wasn't given an opportunity to defend myself. I had other prospects and was able to locate a new position very quickly, so I let the matter drop. Looking back, I regret I didn't make an effort to clear my record for the future.

Otherwise, my work record has been exemplary.

47. Have you ever been asked to resign?

(Now, really. How can someone be asked to resign? You either resign or you're fired! That means you have a choice. And which do you choose? The big R. So the answer should honestly be "No." But if you must answer "Yes," here's how to keep from committing screen-test suicide:)

Yes, from the position of _____ (title) at _____ (name of company) in _____ (year). The request for my resignation arose because my job performance was consistently excellent. My entire department was ready to resign because it disagreed with the management changes taking place, and I had to convince all six employees not to do so at the same time.

_____ (name of company) was constrained by the effects of an unsatisfactory merger and became unresponsive to the changing needs in the marketplace. That was the major cause of their filing for bankruptcy last year. In the meantime, my career has progressed very rapidly upward.

48. What kind of supervisors get the most work from you?

The kind who trust themselves and me—supervisors who are secure in their ability to train people and trust their employees to carry out their responsibilities without exceptions, excuses, or explosions.

By the time we reach the workplace, we should be ready to perform our jobs as mature adults. Most companies have systems for rewarding employees who meet expectations or for reprimanding those who don't. Therefore, a supervisor shouldn't be spending precious management time baby-sitting.

A supervisor's greatest strengths are in the ability to motivate, encourage, and lead others. If the right employees are there, they will respond favorably. The result is a mature relationship of mutual respect where everyone succeeds and the company prospers.

49. Name five reasons for your success.

One, I have high energy and skill levels. As a result, I have a high work output.

Two, I place a strong emphasis on quality, so my work is consistently exceptional.

Three, I continue to improve and polish my skills and abilities. This allows me to increase my contribution to my employer's operations, while at the same time making me feel challenged and fulfilled.

Four, I try to look at old problems from new perspectives and to come up with a creative approach that leads to a workable solution.

Finally, I take responsibility seriously and make it my priority to give an honest day's work for an honest day's pay—every day.

50. Have you ever owned your own business?

(Your own business might have been a T-shirt silk-screening operation run from your dorm in college. Even this seemingly insignificant pursuit is worth mentioning for the points you can score about your organizational, management, and marketing skills.)

Yes, although it wouldn't have made the *Fortune* 500, I'm proud of it. The summer between my sophomore and junior years in college was the summer of 1976—the nation's bicentennial celebration. I had a friend at a design school who asked me to share expenses for an apartment for the summer. The only problem was, neither of us had a job. Because we wanted to be outdoors, we didn't want to spend our summer waiting tables or working behind a counter.

So we teamed up—my friend's art skills with my emerging business skills. She designed and produced beautiful silk-screened T-shirts of tall ships. I handled raw materials, inventory, sales, and bookkeeping. We got a street vendor's license and sold 3,000 shirts in just 10 weeks. Each of us banked almost $4,000 toward the next year's tuition, *after* we paid our rent and other living expenses. We were outdoors, meeting people and having fun by day, then up till the wee hours making more shirts each night. That was fun, too. It was with mixed emotions that we shut down operations two weeks before the semester began so we could lie on the beach and reflect on our success. All in all, it was my favorite summer.

51. How would you rate me as an interviewer?

First, I'd give you high marks for your people skills. You helped me feel at ease right away, which made it easier for me to answer all the questions, even the more difficult ones.

I'd also rate you highly on the creativity of the questions and their thoroughness. Matching the right person to the right job in the right company should be the highest priority. I don't want to be here if it won't result in a successful, long-term relationship. By probing as carefully as you have, you're giving me a better opportunity to secure the most suitable position.

You've given me a complete picture of what to expect at _____ (name of employer), and it confirms my belief that this is where I'd like to work.

Chapter

10

Technology Know-How

DELIVERY

In the past, only people working in very specific fields, such as computer programming, information systems, or engineering, required in-depth knowledge of technology. By the end of the 1980s, however, employers began requiring all job applicants to have some computer skills and training, the level depending on the specific job. Today, all applicants, from cashiers at discount retailers to CEOs at multibillion-dollar firms, are expected to be familiar—if not highly proficient—with many of the technological tools now in widespread use throughout the business world.

Note The questions in this chapter are aimed at helping to prepare job applicants whose work *does not* primarily involve technological know-how. Applicants who work in high-tech areas will need to ensure that they are up to date on their area of expertise, to anticipate the kinds of questions they will be asked.

This chapter cannot begin to address the innumerable questions an individual might be asked during an interview regarding technology. The details of such questions will depend entirely on the particular business area and job requirements. What this chapter does do is to establish a baseline, by posing questions that candidates typically will have to field during a job interview. Most employers today will expect *at least* the level of technological knowledge that these questions address.

SCRIPT

1. **What do you see as the primary impact of computer technology on society in the past ten years?**

On a spectacular scale, computers have enabled people to effect achievements unimaginable only a generation ago: They've helped put people in space, totally altered the way warfare is conducted, solved centuries-old math problems, directed robots to resurrect treasure at the bottom of the sea, and so on. On a more personal level, they've taken over our bookkeeping and telephone chores; ATMs give people the freedom and flexibility to access their money on any day of the week and at any time of the day. In short, computers do anything that can be reduced to numerical or logical operations—an innumerable array of tasks.

2. **Have you been resistant to these changes? Or are you open and enthusiastic about the new technologies?**

To be resistant would be foolhardy. No one who expects to stay competitive and on top of his or her game can afford to deny the inevitable. Computer technology already is a part of all of our lives, even if some of it is behind the scenes and seemingly "out of sight, out of mind."

But am I enthusiastic? I'd call myself a skeptical enthusiast because, historically, when a technological revolution has taken place, the natural tendency is to focus on the positive effects and to marvel at the ingenuity behind the inventions that brought on the revolution. But I've learned through my professional and personal experiences that we never get something without having to give something up, too.

3. What do you see, then, as the advantages and disadvantages of this technology?

The advantages, as I said, are readily apparent. Today, it's difficult for most of us to imagine how the world would function without the help of computerized systems. For example, how could doctors efficiently monitor patients' progress; how could air traffic controllers direct plane traffic; how long would the Gulf War have lasted; what would I do if my car broke down out of town on a Sunday, and I had no cash. The list is endless.

The disadvantages are only just becoming clear, although most of us have already become so accustomed to some of them that we've become passive victims. Who hasn't cursed the absence of a real person on the other end of the phone line when all we have is a simple question? Instead, we're forced to step through endless menus of choices, none of which ever seem to specifically answer our need. and who hasn't spent weeks trying to have a mistake corrected on a bank statement caused by a computer glitch, a hard disk crash, or some other technological mishap? Then there are the physical manifestations of doing so much work on computers: Repetitive stress syndrome is practically epidemic; eyestrain is a given; and everyone complains about neck- and backaches caused by sitting immobile in front of a computer for hours on end.

There is also the problem of standardization: Computer operators are required to interact with many different programs, each of which has many versions. It is difficult to achieve high competency when users are continually expected to absorb new information. Fortunately, learning one program generally makes it easier to learn others.

4. Do you consider yourself computer literate?

(If yes:)

Fortunately, through my work, I've been exposed to various computer applications and systems. In addition, on my own initiative, I have tracked the development of this technology closely. Of course, I don't have hands-on experience with every type of computer or every program—I doubt anyone can say that—but I'm aware of most innovations and highly skilled in several applications.

(If no:)

Although in my most recent position(s) I wasn't offered the opportunity to work on computers or be trained on them, I consider it essential that this capability become part of my skill set. I welcome the challenge and intend to become proficient in this area.

5. What computer platforms and programs are you comfortable using?

(List them, and say how you implement them. The following is a sample response; word yours accordingly.)

I use _____ for example (Word for Windows/the Mac) to prepare all my correspondence and for the text-based portions of my reports. I use (Lotus/1-2-3/Excel) as my spreadsheet programs. And in my current position, I use _____ (QuarkXPress) to produce the company newsletter.

6. In your current position, do you make frequent use of e-mail?

Yes, e-mail has become the primary method of both inter- and intraoffice communication at my company. We use it in lieu of picking up the phone, faxing, and sending memos, to set meetings, stay abreast of the details of projects, and to document our day-to-day activities.

7. Do you consider it to be an effective way to communicate?

It is an incredibly efficient and inexpensive way to send brief memos and urgent notes to colleagues, friends, and family anywhere in the world. Certainly, it's an easy mechanism to document the progression of a project—to create the electronic version of a paper trail.

The downside is that some people have a tendency to overuse it. I've heard colleagues complain of being out of the office for a few days on sick leave or vacation and coming back to find hundreds of e-mail messages awaiting them. That's excessive. E-mail is so easy to use that it's tempting for people to write a new message for each thought they have, rather than organize their comments into a report or lengthier memorandum—or get out of their chairs and take a walk to a colleague's office down the hall. E-mail should be treated as a tool, an aid, not a replacement for all other forms of communication, certainly not for one-on-one human interactions.

8. With so much e-mail flying back and forth, how do you manage to prevent it from intruding on work that you need to focus on for long periods of time?

I control it; I don't let it control me, by which I mean I set times during my workday to check my e-mail. I don't stop what I'm doing every time the e-mail program alerts me that I have a new message. Otherwise, I'd never get anything done.

9. Do you find the Internet and the World Wide Web to be of value in your daily work? If so, how?

Absolutely—at the very least for research purposes. It is almost always more time efficient to look up a fact or detail on the Internet than to consult paper-based sources. In addition, I keep abreast of my company's competitors on the Web, checking out their web sites on a regular basis to track any advances they're making or new directions they're heading. This is proving essential to doing my job effectively.

10. Do you have a computer at home? If so, do you have an Internet account?

(If yes:)

Having a computer at home gives me more flexibility in my work. Instead of staying late at the office to finish an important project, I can come home, relax a little, and get back to work, refreshed and reenergized. It also enables me to work with colleagues in different time zones all over the world, if need be.

I also use my home computer to track my personal expenses, to take care of personal correspondence, and to indulge my outside pursuits, both recreational and educational.

(If appropriate:)

My home computer is also an excellent way of interacting with my children, who like all other kids today, are very computer savvy. Not only has our home computer made it easier for my children to do homework and research, but it's made the entire world available to us, to explore together.

(If no:)

I plan to _____ (purchase/update) a computer system _____ (before year's end/in the next six months). I am in the process of educating myself—comparison-shopping and doing research—to determine what platform I prefer and what would be most appropriate for my household.

11. What are your thoughts about the various controversies surrounding such widespread use of the Internet, specifically issues concerning misuse, abuse, privacy, and copyright?

Every technological advance in history has become the target of unscrupulous people who find ways to corrupt it for unsavory, even criminal, purposes: a case in point is the telephone, which since its inception has been controversial because of wiretapping, obscene phone callers, intrusive telemarketers, and so on. These problems continue to confound regulators more than 100 years after the invention of the telephone.

In short, there is no easy answer for how to handle the disadvantages that come with the many advantages offered by the Internet. Probably, answers will be found on an as-needed basis, depending on public demand and both private and government willingness and determination to find workable solutions. Some will probably be adaptations of current laws to a new format, such as seems to be happening with issues of copyright. Other solutions will come from the private sector, such as filter programs that enable parents to monitor and/or block their children's access to certain aspects of the Internet. In the meantime, individuals must take responsibility for themselves and those in their care.

12. The rapid pace of change in technology today is unparalleled. How do you stay up to date?

I doubt anyone can be truly knowledgeable about all the technology on the market today; probably it's not necessary. What is necessary is to stay informed about the tools and programs that impact how I do my job. To that end, I make an effort to read the technology news in the paper; and I regularly read at least one of the many magazines devoted to these topics. Of course, the Web is an excellent source of the latest news of technological advances.

13. **Some people always seem to be connected to one gadget or another. Is there such a thing as too much technology?**

It depends; I can understand that a salesperson, for example, would really benefit by having a cell phone, a Palm Pilot, and a laptop computer with him or her at all times. Competition is tough out there, and being up to date at all times can mean the difference between success and failure.

On the personal side, I'd have to say the same: It depends—whether a person's idea of relaxation is spending his or her free time on the Web, playing games, being a member of a chat community, and so on, or unplugging it all and going for a walk in the country or reading a good book.

Though the media hype would make it seem otherwise, the truth is, we still have a choice as to whether technology runs us or we run technology.

Chapter

11

Outside
Interests

DELIVERY

If you were applying at a dating service, this would be an important area. Otherwise, your outside interests don't affect your ability to do your job. However, for the time being, you do have an important *inside* interest: delivering your script and successfully passing this final part of the screen test.

So, if the company is really big on charity drives, mention your assistance to charities. If it encourages employees to participate in civic activities, mention that. Most people have enough outside interests they can convert to inside interests as soon as the curtain rises.

How do successful interviewees learn how to answer these questions? Through keen powers of observation. Before they ever enter the interviewer's office, they've scoped out the company's offices and made mental notes of trophies, awards, citations, photos, and any other physical clues that reveal what is important to the company. Earlier phone sleuthing might have revealed information about company trips, picnics, and blood drives as well.

I was a personnel manager for a company that wouldn't hire anyone who didn't lift weights. Was it discriminatory? Yes. Was it unfair? Yes. Was it ridiculous? Yes. Was it legal? Yes.

Did I liberalize the definition of "lifting weights" for otherwise qualified applicants? Yes.

SCRIPT

1. How interested are you in sports?

I like playing them more than watching them. Some require mental discipline. Some require a cooperative team effort. But all reward those who are the best.

Sports are sometimes violent and unproductive, but they can also teach valuable lessons. If someone doesn't have much self-esteem, sports can help him or her develop into a high achiever. The message is that hard work can pay off. In sports, people learn their limitations, too. No one can be best at everything. Learning your weaknesses can help you develop your strengths.

2. What are your leisure-time activities?

(Before answering this question, conduct a split-second mental review of the clues you picked up on your way in. If this company appears to be activity-oriented, and you play racquetball but also collect stamps, emphasize racquetball. If you know something about the company culture—an emphasis on family values, for example—concentrate on that aspect of your life.)

My dedication to my career takes up most of my time. However, I make it a point to spend time with my family every day. I'm involved in my kids' sports and help them with their homework. After that, I settle down and catch up on my work-related reading—journals and other trade publications.

Weekends are spent in family activities, gardening, social events, and community affairs.

(Now, your answer:)

_____

_____

_____

_____.

3. **What were your extracurricular activities in school?**

(If the target job requires leadership skills, accent your leadership activities. If physical stamina and conditioning are required, mention your sports achievements. If it is a people-oriented occupation, tell about community involvement.)

I was captain of the debating team and vice-president of the senior class. My extracurricular activities in school served to guide me in my career choices. Leadership roles, where effective communication is required, come naturally to me.

OR

My extracurricular activities in high school and college centered around sports—mainly football and track. Being active and staying in top physical condition are still important to me, because they make me more effective in everything I do.

(Now, your answer:)

_____

_____

_____

_____

_____

_____.

4. What newspaper do you read? What section do you turn to first?

(Customize your answer to reflect the job. "News" is always a safe answer; but the business section is a good second stop for a business manager, and the commentary section is important for someone involved in government.)

I read the _Wall Street Journal_ because it gives me a quick synopsis of international news and allows me to focus on economic trends that are important in my work. On Sundays I read our local weekend paper to catch up on community affairs, local business activity, and commentary.

(Now, your answer:)

_____

_____

_____

_____

_____

_____.

5. What is your favorite television program?

(Just try answering *"Wheel of Fortune"* or *"I Love Lucy"* reruns, and see how fast the spotlights go out and the curtain falls. Answer *"Masterpiece Theater"* and you might be labeled too highbrow. Try to chart a middle course.)

There isn't much time in my life for watching television, other than the evening news. Occasionally, I see if there's something interesting to watch. I like business-oriented specials and news features the best.

6. Can you name the U.S. senators from your state?

(Be sure you can. If you don't know them, look them up now and write them here.)

Of course. The senior senator is _____ _____, a (Republican/Democrat), and the junior senator is _____, a (Republican/ Democrat).

7. Have you ever been the head of a committee?

(This is a good chance to mention community leadership and organization experience. Even if you haven't participated in recent years, see if you can find something to score a few extra points.)

Yes, several times. Most recently, I chaired the annual fund-raising event for _____, a local service club. I've headed up several different committees for that organization in past years.

I had a great deal of leadership experience as a teenager as well. I was actively involved in youth fund-raising efforts for the March of Dimes and other causes, often taking a leadership role.

Citizenship means more than paying taxes and keeping your yard clean. I try to get involved and assist whenever I can.

8. Do you consider yourself a social drinker?

(A moderate answer is your best bet here. You have no way of knowing, but the company might prohibit any alcohol use by employees during working hours. Or you might be in the midst of a real office-party culture where nondrinkers are ostracized.)

I enjoy an occasional glass of wine with a formal dinner. But I can take or leave alcohol in social situations. At business functions where clients are present, if I drink at all, it will be just one drink so I will be sure to stay alert and represent the company to the best of my ability.

9. Does your social life include associates and co-workers?

From time to time, it has. I have many outside interests, however, and many friends that I know through them.

I enjoy company functions, but my social life doesn't revolve around work. I prefer to strike a good balance between my personal and professional activities. It's easier to handle difficult situations with co-workers when they aren't good friends.

This professional detachment doesn't mean you can't be sensitive to the needs of others. It just makes the relationship more objective and businesslike. We're being paid to do a job—there's really not much time for socializing when we're doing it.

10. Have you ever received an award or citation?

(Many of us tend to forget the awards, certificates, and other recognition we've received for work-related and outside activities. Think carefully about this answer, then list any recognition in the blanks provided:)

Yes, I was named _____ by the _____ in _____ (year), and I received the _____ award in _____ for _____

_____

_____.

11. What kind of jobs did you have as a child?

My parents encouraged responsibility from an early age. I was assigned household chores from the age of

_____ and began helping with the family business at the age of _____.

In addition, my entrepreneurial spirit surfaced early. I had lemonade stands, rummage sales, and backyard plays. Also, I was the first kid outside with snowsuit and shovel after a snowfall, knocking on neighbors' doors to clear their driveways for a dollar.

12. What are you doing to improve yourself?

Self-improvement should be part of everyone's life. I educate myself informally through reading. I try to learn something new on a regular basis by reading an article on an unfamiliar topic. I also review self-help techniques in books and magazines. It keeps me sharp.

(If applicable:)

I'm presently taking a course in _____ at _____ as well.

Beyond that, I maintain optimum health through regular exercise and proper diet, and I follow a routine of

_____

_____.

13. What do you plan to do to improve yourself?

In the future, I plan to _____

_____

(return to school to get a master's degree/finish my bachelor's degree/take courses in _____) _____

_____ .

Beyond that, I'll continue developing myself every day, both on the job and off. That's what makes life worthwhile—the striving for excellence, to be the best you can be.

14. What is the most interesting trip you have ever taken?

My work and community responsibilities have kept me too busy to take extended trips to exotic places, but a fascinating trip was to _____

_____ .

I've particularly enjoyed family weekend trips. One of the most interesting was a trip to _____ in _____ .

Of course, business trips are a great learning experience, too. They're interesting as well, particularly when they've been successful!

Chapter

12

Questions to Ask the Interviewer

DELIVERY

Although they don't require great acting ability to deliver, asking appropriate questions demonstrates your interest in the job. It also gives you the opportunity to lead the interviewer into your strongest areas.

Your questions and the interviewer's answers shouldn't exceed 10 percent of the total interview time. Because you don't know how long the interview will last, just ask a question after you have answered around nine of them. Don't sit there writing tally marks on your resume, just mentally keep track. If you ask two questions, wait a little longer before you ask about something else.

Questioning must be done naturally at opportune times, and in a nonthreatening manner. No question should be asked unless you are certain the answer will make you appear *interested, intelligent,* and *qualified.*

Proper questioning helps you align *your* answers to the areas the interviewer considers significant. It also gives you feedback to check your alignment. Listen for company and industry buzzwords to use as the interview progresses. Above all, don't interrupt or argue with the interviewer. You're asking only to be able to play to your audience more effectively, not to rate or berate it.

The average applicant talks about 85 percent of the time during an interview. That's why average applicants don't get hired. They're amateur solo acts with monotonous monologues who nervously bang their gums on the interviewer's drums. Then both of them march out the door together, and only the interviewer returns.

Applicants who get hired zip the lip 50 percent of the time. This is one of the most accurate indicators of whether an offer will be extended—and *you* can control it.

Use questions as zippers to help you. Don't ask personal, controversial, or negative questions of any kind. Stay away from asking anything that will lead into sensitive areas. Invariably, salary and benefits should be avoided—I've shown you how to answer properly the interviewer's questions about them.

Here are examples of benign questions that have a favorable impact, adapted from *The Placement Strategy Handbook*:

SCRIPT

1. How many employees does the company have?

2. What are the company's plans for expansion?

3. How many employees does the department have?

4. Is the department a profit center?

5. Does the department work separately from other departments?

6. Are the functions of the department important to senior management?

7. Is the relationship between the department and senior management favorable?

8. What is the supervisor's management style?

9. What is the supervisor's title?

10. To whom does the supervisor report?

11. Are you ready and able to hire now?

12. How long will it take to make a hiring decision?

13. How long has the position been open?

14. How many employees have held the position in the past five years?

15. Why are the former employees no longer in the position?

16. How many employees have been promoted from the position in the past five years?

17. What does the company consider the five most important duties of the position?

18. What do you expect the employee you hire to accomplish?

BENEFITS QUESTIONS

Though, of course, you will need—and have a right—to ask the following questions, the key is knowing when to do so. Under no circumstances do you want to spring these questions on the interviewer early in your conversation; doing so will make it seem as if you were more interested in what the company can do for you, when at this juncture what you want to get across is what you can do for the company.

The best advice for raising these questions is to have them firmly in mind so that you can ask them at the appropriate times during the interview. And if you've followed all the advice so far in the book, you will know when these times are. In general, however, many of these questions will probably be part of the salary negotiation process (see Chapter 8).

1. **What type of medical insurance benefits program does the company offer? Is more than one type of program available?**

[Be sure to follow the first question with questions 2 and 3.]

2. **What is the extent of the coverage of the program [*or various programs, if more than one*]?**

3. **Does the company pay for the coverage in whole, or must the employee contribute? If the latter, what percentage?**

4. **What is the sick leave policy?**

5. What is the vacation benefit for this position?

6. Is it possible to join a retirement plan? If so, is it contributory or noncontributory?

7. Does the company have a profit-sharing plan? Is documentation of its payout history available?

8. Is there a 401k plan? If so, how is it structured?

9. Are there other savings or investment programs employees can choose from?

10. Will the company arrange for and pay for my moving expenses?

11. [In the case of a homeowner] Will the company assist in the sale of my current home and the search and purchase of my new home? Does the company reimburse closing costs on these transactions?

12. [In the case of a renter] If my landlord is unwilling to release me from the time remaining on my lease, will the company assume the balance of the monthly payments for the extent of the lease?

13. Will the company help with real estate loans, if necessary? If so, under what terms?

Index

About the Author

Jeffrey G. Allen, J.D., C.P.C., is the nation's foremost authority on the interview process. His first book, *How to Turn an Interview into a Job*, has been a bestseller for over a decade. Several years later he wrote another bestseller, *The Complete Q&A Job Interview Book*. Its continued popularity has resulted in this new, updated edition. The most popular books in the *Jeff Allen's Best* series are *Get the Interview* and *Win the Job*. His *Get Hired! System* was the first audio program for jobseekers.

Jeff has written more bestselling books in the career field than anyone else. He was a recruiter and human resources manager, served as special advisor to the American Employment Association, and is an honorary member of the California Association of Personnel Consultants.

As a leading employment attorney, certified placement counselor, and certified employment specialist, Jeff is uniquely qualified to be your interacting coach.

He can be reached regarding legal matters at:

Law Offices of Jeffrey G. Allen
9601 Wilshire Boulevard
Suite 1400
Beverly Hills, CA 90210
(310) 559-6000